the content maker's handbook

Philip Alberstat

Copyright © 2017 by Philip Alberstat

All rights reserved. No part of this book may be reproduced or transmitted in any form or by any means, electronic or mechanical, including photocopying, recording, or by any information storage and retrieval system, without permission in writing from the copyright owner. This is a work of fiction. Names, characters, places and incidents either are the product of the author's imagination or are used fictitiously, and any resemblance to any actual persons, living or dead, events, or locales is entirely coincidental.

This book was printed in the United States of America. To order additional copies of this book, contact: Info at *psa@49northmedia.com*

This book is for Erika, Thea, Ally, Evie, Levi,
Margot and Stephanie.
Thanks for all the intelligence, humor and love.

DISCLAIMER

This book is designed to help non-lawyers understand many of the legal and production issues that are frequently encountered in the content creation business. The chapters and sample agreements should be used as a guide to understand the law and help content creators to communicate better with their attorney. Nothing in this book should be construed as legal advice and is not a substitute for the advice of qualified counsel. The facts and circumstances of a production are all different and therefore content creators should always consult with their attorney. The sample agreements in this book will always need to be tailored and modified to fit the specific circumstances of each production.

Table of Contents

Introduction 7

CHAPTER 1   Mutual Non-Disclosure Agreement (NDA) 11

CHAPTER 2   Rights Shopping Agreement 19

CHAPTER 3   Freelance Crew Agreement 27

CHAPTER 4   Social Media Influencer Agreement 43

CHAPTER 5   Personal Release – All Rights 69

CHAPTER 6   Crowd Release 75

CHAPTER 7   Location License Agreement 79

CHAPTER 8   Artwork Release Form 97

CHAPTER 9   Composer Agreement 101

CHAPTER 10   Music License 107

CHAPTER 11   Sample Call Sheet 115

Introduction

Online video has become the go-to place for people to satisfy their information and entertainment needs. Video is everywhere. Some estimate that people post 400 hours of video on YouTube every minute and watch nearly 7 million Snapchat videos in the same period. Facebook in 2016 claims to have video views of 100 million hours a day and Instagram video viewing continues to grow at a furious pace. Consumers continue to increase their engagement with mobile devices for daily activities and content consumption. By the end of 2017 it is claimed that video will account for almost 70% of all consumer internet traffic.

With the growth of video consumption there has been many viral video success stories. These viral videos have shown video's inherent share-ability. What these videos prove is that if an audience is engaged they will share them with others. Psy's Gangnam Style and Charlie Bit My Finger are examples of videos with hundreds of millions of views. The share-ability factor has forced companies to think about video as a key element in reaching consumers. Companies that are creating successful videos have been able to prove that people will spend longer on their website and more time interacting with their brand. Small and large businesses have now embraced video and are now including it as a key part of their internet marketing strategies.

Now that companies are embracing the online world for their marketing needs, we are now seeing advertising spending patterns change. According to e-Marketer, in 2017 total digital ad spending in the United States will equal $77.4 Billion or 38.5% of all advertising spending. Television will be at $72Billion or 35.8% of total media ad spending. Some feel that online video will continue to grow and overtake television spending in the near future.

What does this all mean? This means that there is a huge demand for more and more video. This will translate in to a massive opportunity for content creators to satisfy this need for video. Not only have advertising spending patterns changed but production costs have fallen significantly in recent years because of developments in cameras, apps and editing technology. The barriers to entry for content creators is very low and almost anyone can create content with easily accessible professional cameras or their smartphones. The production process for feature films and long form television remains highly labor intensive and complex whereas short form video production for online consumption can be relatively simple. However, as more companies engage professional content creators we are now seeing bigger budgets and higher expectations for better video product. This will mean that content creators from students to influencers will need to follow a certain process to ensure that the final product they create is able to be viewed without the fear of any legal threat.

The order of the chapters in the book have been arranged based the experience I have had in the production process at the company I co-founded in 2014. In our early days, we were a scrappy production company making videos for many household brands. These brands had low budgets and very urgent deadlines. What is interesting is that years later, the budgets are still low and the deadlines still urgent. However, even with the larger budgets and longer deadlines, the process is still the same.

The process generally starts when a brand sends a non-disclosure agreement, (NDA) so they can brief you on the type of content they are looking for. In many cases a brand will send a request for proposal also referred to as an RFP. RFP's come in many forms but they generally are a creative brief that gives a producer some background information on the brand or specific product, the objective that the brand is trying to accomplish, a target audience, the actual assignment, deliverables, creative requirements, timing and budget. If you succeed in winning the work then the production process begins.

The chapters in the book are arranged in an order that follows the production process. Hiring creative people, crew and influencers are some of the initial steps which are then followed by actual physical production. Various releases and agreements are contained in the book that will help content creators understand some of the specific needs of a production.

One goal of this book is to help content creators understand the production process from ideation to final delivery of their content. Each chapter of the book will guide content creators through important steps of the ideation and production process. The chapters provide guidance and highlight important legal issues in the various contractual relationships that are required when making content. The agreements in the book are samples for informational purposes. It is essential to have a knowledgeable attorney who specializes in media and entertainment law to provide professional advice.

CHAPTER 1

MUTUAL NON-DISCLOSURE AGREEMENT (NDA)

Non-Disclosure (NDA) Agreement Chapter Notes

A non-disclosure agreement(NDA) is also sometimes referred to as a confidentiality agreement. The purpose of the agreement is to create a legal obligation to privacy and compels those who agree to keep any information disclosed secret. NDA's are very common in many business settings including content development and production since they offer a straightforward way to protect trade secrets or other confidential information. The types of information that a content business may want to keep secret can include, treatments, scripts, client information such as a brand or the type of new product they may be launching and any other sensitive information that could potentially cause some harm.

NDA's need to be clear on what they are covering. Certain elements in the agreement such as the definitions and exclusions of what is confidential information are important to define. The agreement should define exactly what type of information is included. For example, if a production company is sharing information with a potential video director about a new product launch for a client, then the NDA should be very specific about this and be very descriptive of what needs to be protected.

The NDA should also be very specific about the type of information that is excluded. Information that is usually excluded includes, information that is publicly known or in the public domain, information obtained already from third parties or already obtained by the recipient.

The NDA should also be very specific about the length of time they are in force. Most agreements cover a 6 month–2-year period where information needs to be kept confidential. The period of time depends on the strategic value of the information and how quickly the information may become obsolete.

Another important consideration is whether the NDA is mutual, meaning both parties sign it and both parties keep what they divulge to each other secret. Alternatively, an NDA may only be one way, whereby the company divulging information ensures that the receiving party keeps that information private.

THIS AGREEMENT IS FOR TEACHING PURPOSES ONLY

MUTUAL NON-DISCLOSURE AGREEMENT

This Mutual Non-Disclosure Agreement ("**Agreement**") is made as of { DATE} ,201_ (the "**Effective Date**") between PRODUCTION COMPANY and its directly or indirectly wholly-owned subsidiaries ("**Production Company**") on one hand and the participant identified below ("**Participant**") on the other.

1. Definition. "Confidential Information" means information relating to the Discloser's business, including, without limitation, product designs, product plans, data, software and technology, financial information, marketing plans, business opportunities, proposed terms, pricing information, discounts, inventions and know-how disclosed by Discloser to Recipient, either directly or indirectly, whether in writing, verbally or otherwise, and whether prior to, on or after the Effective Date, that either: (a) is designated as confidential by the Discloser at the time of disclosure; or (b) would reasonably be understood, given the nature of the information or the circumstances surrounding its disclosure, to be confidential. Confidential Information also includes the existence of this Agreement and the fact or nature of the discussions between the parties.

2. Use of Confidential Information. A party which receives Confidential Information under this Agreement ("**Recipient**") may use the Confidential Information only to evaluate whether to enter into a business relationship with the party which discloses Confidential Information under this Agreement ("**Discloser**").

3. **Disclosure of Confidential Information.** Recipient will: (a) hold Confidential Information in strict confidence and take reasonable precautions to protect such Confidential Information (such precautions to include, at a minimum, all precautions Recipient employs with respect to its own confidential materials); (b) not divulge any Confidential Information to any third party (other than to employees or contractors as set forth below); and (c) not copy or reverse engineer any materials disclosed under this Agreement or remove any proprietary markings from any Confidential Information. Any employee or contractor given access to any Confidential Information must have a legitimate "need to know" such Confidential Information for use specified in Section 2 and Recipient will remain responsible for each such person's compliance with the terms of this Agreement.

4. **Term; Confidentiality Period.** Either party may terminate this Agreement upon 30 days prior written notice to the other party. Irrespective of any termination of this Agreement, Recipient's obligations with respect to Confidential Information under this Agreement expire 2 years from the date of receipt of the Confidential Information (except with respect to any trade secrets where such obligations will be perpetual).

5. **Exclusions.** This Agreement imposes no obligations with respect to information which: (a) was in Recipient's possession before receipt from Discloser; (b) is or becomes a matter of public knowledge through no fault of Recipient; (c) was rightfully disclosed to Recipient by a third party without restriction on disclosure; or (d) is developed by

Recipient without use of the Confidential Information as can be shown by documentary evidence. Recipient may make disclosures to the extent required by law or court order provided Recipient makes commercially reasonable efforts to provide Discloser with notice of such disclosure as promptly as possible and uses diligent efforts to limit such disclosure and obtain confidential treatment or a protective order and has allowed Discloser to participate in the proceeding.

6. Return or Destruction of Confidential Information. Upon termination of this Agreement or written request by Discloser, the Recipient will: (a) cease using the Confidential Information; (b) return or destroy the Confidential Information and all copies, notes or extracts thereof to Discloser within 7 business days of receipt of request; and (c) upon request of Discloser, confirm in writing that Recipient has complied with these obligations.

7. Proprietary Rights. Neither party to this Agreement acquires any intellectual property rights nor any other rights under this Agreement except the limited right to use the Confidential Information set forth in Section 2.

8. Disclaimer. CONFIDENTIAL INFORMATION IS PROVIDED "AS IS" AND WITH ALL FAULTS.

9. Publicity. Neither party will make, or authorize any third party to make, any public announcement or other disclosures related to this Agreement and any potential agreement or relationship with the other party or any of its affiliates or subsidiaries without the prior written approval of the other party. For the purposes of this Agreement public announcements include disclosures to any person or entity other than the Recipient by any means, including but not limited to, press releases, written or oral statements made to the media, blogs, trade organizations, publications, websites, or any other public audience or unauthorized third parties.

10. Export. Recipient agrees not to remove or export any such Confidential Information or any direct product thereof, except in compliance with, and with all applicable export laws and regulation.

11. Injunctive Relief. Each party acknowledges that any breach of this Agreement may cause irreparable harm for which monetary damages are an insufficient remedy and therefore that upon any breach of this Agreement Discloser will be entitled to appropriate equitable relief without the posting of a bond in addition to whatever remedies it might have at law.

12. General. Neither party has an obligation under this Agreement to purchase or offer for sale any item or proceed with any proposed transaction. In the event that any of the provisions of this Agreement will be held illegal or unenforceable by a court of competent jurisdiction, such provisions will be limited or eliminated to the minimum extent necessary so that this Agreement will otherwise remain in full force and effect. Neither party may assign this Agreement without the prior written consent of the other party. This Agreement will be governed by the laws of the State of California and the United States without regard to conflicts of laws provisions thereof. This Agreement supersedes all prior discussions and writings and constitutes the entire agreement between the parties with respect to the subject matter hereof. The prevailing party in any action to enforce this Agreement will be entitled to costs and attorneys' fees. No waiver or modification of this Agreement will be binding upon either party unless made in writing and signed by a duly authorized representative of each party and no failure or delay in enforcing any right will be deemed a waiver.

ACKNOWLEDGED AND AGREED:

Production Company	Participant: _____
Signature: _____	Signature: _____
Name: _____	Name: _____
Title: _____	Title: _____
Address:	Address:

CHAPTER 2

RIGHTS SHOPPING AGREEMENT

Rights Shopping Agreement
Chapter Notes

A Shopping Agreement is a contract that is heavily used in the film and television industry which allows a producer to exclusively "shop" a film or television project to potential end users such as a financier, studio or network for a certain period of time.

Shopping agreements are now being used by content creators in the short form and brand content space on a much more frequent basis to "shop" projects to companies and various platforms that need content.

The agreement offers producers a no-cost way of attaching themselves to a project and obtaining the right to pitch the project to potential buyers. Under a shopping agreement the copyright owner retains all rights and ownership in the project whereas in a traditional option agreement a producer will set out the purchase terms in advance for a small fee for a certain period. Under a shopping agreement, if the producer sets up a deal with a potential end user, then the producer and copyright owner will each negotiate their own deals.

The agreement has benefits for both the producer and copyright owner as it is a quick way to avoid lengthy negotiations and legal expenses that are usually required for an option agreement. If the producer fails to set up a deal with someone during the agreed period both parties can walk away. However, most shopping agreements have a post term clause whereby if the producer has submitted a project to a potential buyer during the term of the agreement then for a certain period (for example 12 months) after expiry of the agreement the copyright owner cannot set the project up without the producer's involvement with the same buyer.

THE CONTENT MAKER'S HANDBOOK

In the fast paced world of content creation, producers may want to utilize the speed and efficiency of a shopping agreement when they come across great stories and projects that they want to try and set up quickly.

SHOPPING AGREEMENT

From:- [NAME/ADDRESS OF PRODUCTION COMPANY/PRODUCER]
TO:- [NAME OF RIGHTS OWNER}

RE: [NAME OF PROJECT]

Dear [NAME]

This letter shall confirm the terms of the agreement ("Agreement") between us as follows:

1. Reference is made to the following:

   (a) You represent and warrant that you own and control the motion picture, television, digital and related rights to the [magazine/newspaper/online article ,NEED TO DESCRIBE THE TYPE OF UNDERLYING WORK] entitled "NAME OF PROJECT/UNDERLYING RIGHTS" (the "Property").

   (b) You are now prepared to option, sell and/or license such rights in and to the Property for the purpose of advancing the production, distribution, and exploitation of one or more motion pictures and/or television productions and/or digital productions based on the Property (collectively the "Project").

2. For good and valuable consideration (including, without limitation, my time and creative contributions to the Project), the receipt and sufficiency of which is hereby

acknowledged by you, you have agreed that beginning as of the date above and continuing thereafter for a period of eighteen (18) months from the date of full execution of this Agreement (the "Term") (which Term shall be automatically extended in the event that the development of the Project is interfered with or interrupted by an event of force majeure (as commonly understood in the entertainment industry), a claim is asserted that (if proved) would constitute a breach by you of this Agreement, and/or prior to the end of the Term we are in active negotiations with a Production Entity (as defined below) with respect to the Project (provided, however, any such extension due to on-going negotiations with a Production Entity shall be capped at ninety (90) days)), I will be irrevocably attached as the executive producer of the Project.

3. During the Term, I shall have the exclusive right to engage in customary development activities with respect to the Project including, without limitation, soliciting actors, directors, and others for participation in the Project; submitting the Project to any third party entities including, but not limited to, studios, networks, financiers and production companies ("Production Entity(ies)") for further production / financing / distribution; publicizing the Project and my involvement therewith; and engaging in any other relevant activities that I deem necessary or desirable to develop and obtain financing for the Project. You shall have no right, title or interest in the results and proceeds of such development and pre-production activities and all such development materials (including, without limitation, any screenplays written) shall be and remain my sole and exclusive property. During the Term, you shall not attach any other elements to the Project or solicit the Project to any third parties including, without limitation, Production Entities, without my prior written consent.

4. If, during the Term, a Production Entity wishes to enter into negotiations for the possible development, production, distribution and/or other exploitation of the Project, we shall individually negotiate our own deals with such Production Entity for our respective rights and services on the Project (for the avoidance of doubt, for the services of [NAME OF PRODUCER] as the executive producer of the Project and [NAME OF PRODUCTION COMPANY] as the primary production company, and for your motion picture and related rights in and to the Property and any other services that may be required of you by such Production Entity). Neither of us shall enter into an agreement with such Production Entity with respect to the Project unless and until the other is ready to conclude an agreement with such Production Entity in connection with the Project. We agree to act reasonably and in good faith with respect to such negotiations consistent with the budget of the Project, industry standard, our precedents and in a manner that will not frustrate our intent to develop, finance and produce the Project.

5. During the Term, you shall not (a) produce, or authorize the production of, any production based on the Property and/or the Project unless produced upon the terms hereof; (b) enter into any agreements with a Production Entity or any other third party regarding the Property and/or the Project unless consistent with the terms hereof; and (c) assign or transfer all or any part of your rights in the Property or obligations under this Agreement to any person or entity (other than to a Production Entity provided I have concluded my deal pursuant to Paragraph 4 above) without my express prior written consent.

6. You agree that for a period of twelve (12) months following the expiration of the Term, if any Production Entity to which the Project was submitted prior to expiration of the Term,

including those with which negotiations were started and terminated, desires to enter into negotiations regarding the possible financing, development or production of the Project, the provisions of this Agreement shall apply.

7. Our working relationship applies to this Project only. Subject to the terms of this Agreement, we shall be free to take any other engagements and otherwise arrange our schedules until such time, if ever, as a firm and binding fully executed and funded pay-or-play agreement is concluded.

8. This Agreement constitutes the entire understanding between us with regard to the Project and may not be amended or modified except in a writing signed by both of us, and shall be binding upon and inure to the benefit of each of us and our heirs, successors and assigns. We agree that in entering into this Agreement we have not relied upon any promise or representation not contained in this Agreement and that this Agreement supersedes any prior discussions and/or agreements between us with respect to the subject matter hereof. We agree that the state and federal courts in Los Angeles County, California shall have personal jurisdiction over us, and will be the exclusive forum for any disputes arising out of this Agreement, and that California law will apply. In the event of any action or proceeding arising hereunder, the prevailing party shall be entitled to its reasonable outside attorneys' fees and costs. This Agreement may be executed in any number of counterparts which, when taken as a whole, shall constitute one valid and binding original and a photocopy of a signature or a facsimile copy of a signature shall be treated as an original. You acknowledge that you have carefully read this Agreement and that you have had the right to consult legal counsel concerning this Agreement.

If the foregoing accurately reflects our agreement, please sign this deal letter where indicated below.

Sincerely,
NAME OF PRODUCTION COMPANY

By:

Its:

Dated: _____

ACCEPTED AND AGREED:

_____
NAME OF RIGHTS OWNER

Dated: _____

CHAPTER 3

FREELANCE CREW AGREEMENT

Freelance Crew Agreement- Chapter Notes

Many video productions are created by companies that use freelance crews. Production companies will have full time producers or a head of production and will engage individual crew members depending on the size of a video shoot. The Freelance Crew Agreement in this chapter can be used for a variety of roles on a video shoot. Director, camera operator, costume designer, make-up artist and any other role that is needed. The headings in the agreement are self-explanatory but producers engaging freelance crew should always consider the following.

Always be very clear with the person you are engaging about what you want them to do. In this agreement, there is plenty of room to be very descriptive of the job the person is being asked to do.

How long do you need the person? No one likes to work for free. Be very clear about the days for prep, shoot and any post work. In some cases, you may want to agree a half day or full day rate. It is also important to make it clear that you can fire someone from the production and what happens when you terminate them. Most agreements ask that you give 24 hours notice to terminate someone. Once terminated you will need to pay them for any work they have done.

How much will they be paid? This follows on from above. Agree a half day, day rate or a rate for the entire shoot. It is also important to be clear when the person is paid. Usually a freelance crew person is paid within a week of them submitting an invoice. Most production companies who engage freelance crew will also ask for the appropriate tax forms to be filled out by the person providing services.

Insurance is always an issue to consider. Producers will need to make sure that freelance crew are covered by their production insurance policy. Also, if a crew member is bringing their own equipment such as a camera or sound equipment then it is essential that you understand if they have their own insurance for their gear. If not then you will need to discuss coverage with your production insurance carrier.

This agreement makes it very clear that anyone working on your production is providing their services as a "work for hire" and that all the rights in the work they do is owned by the production company. It is also important if someone from the crew appears on camera that you obtain the rights to use their image.

Confidentiality is always a concern when doing work for brands that may be launching a new product or service. If this is the case then you will need to make it clear in the agreement that no photography or social media posts are allowed on the set and any scripts or materials provided remain the property of the production company.

FREELANCE CREW AGREEMENT

Freelance Service
Provider Legal Name: _____

  Billing Address: _____

  Phone/Fax/Email: _____

  Client: _____Description of Services_____

  Effective Date: _____

This **FREELANCE CREW AGREEMENT** (this "Agreement"), dated as of the Effective Date, between [NAME OF PRODUCTION COMPANY], whose address is [ADDRESS] ("PRODUCER"), and the Freelance Service Provider named above ("Service Provider"). Producer and the Service Provider may individually be referred to as a "Party" and collectively as the "Parties." In consideration of the agreements, covenants, representations and warranties contained in this Agreement, Service Provider and Producer agree as follows:

ARTICLE I : SERVICES; TERM; TERMINATION

Section 1.1   Services. During the Term, and in accordance with the provisions contained in this Agreement, Producer hereby appoints Service Provider to provide the services described on Exhibit A attached hereto ("Services"). Any change, addition or reduction to the scope of Services must be agreed upon in writing.

Section 1.2   Term; Termination. This Agreement shall commence on the Effective Date and shall expire when the Services are completed by Service Provider in accordance with the terms of this Agreement, unless sooner terminated in accordance with the provisions of this Agreement ("Term"). This Agreement may be terminated by Producer, without penalty, by delivering twenty-four (24) hours' prior written notice thereof to Service Provider. This Agreement may be terminated by Service Provider by delivering thirty (30) days' prior written notice to Producer. Any provision of this Agreement which imposes an obligation after the termination of this Agreement shall survive the termination of this Agreement.

Section 1.3   Effect of Early Termination. Upon the termination of this Agreement for any reason, Service Provider shall (a) cease providing Services for Producer and promptly return all Confidential Information to Producer, and (b) Producer shall reimburse Service Provider for any documented costs and expenses incurred on or before the effective date of termination of this Agreement.

ARTICLE II: FEES AND PAYMENT

Section 2.1   Fees and Expenses. In accordance with the provisions of this Agreement, Producer shall pay Service Provider the fees described on Exhibit A ("Fees"). Unless otherwise expressly set forth in Exhibit A, Service Provider shall be responsible for all costs and expenses Service Provider incurs in connection with the performance of the Services.

Section 2.2   Invoicing and Payment. Service Provider shall deliver to Producer within [ ] days of completion of the Services all invoices for Fees to Producer. Producer shall pay all amounts within [ ] days of Producer's receipt of each invoice.

SECTION III: AGREEMENTS AND COVENANTS

Section 3.1   Service Provider Equipment. Service Provider agrees that Producer shall not be liable for, and expressly waives all rights, if any, to assert any claims against Producer and any of its Affiliates (as defined below), agents, employees, directors, officers, contractors or representatives for any damage to any property of Service Provider occurring before, during or after Service Provider's performance of the Services.

Section 3.2   Subcontracting; Removal of Personnel. Service Provider shall not engage a subcontractor to perform any of the Services without obtaining the prior written consent of Producer. If Producer approves a subcontractor presented by Service Provider, Service Provider agrees that it shall obligate such subcontractor to adhere to and be bound by an agreement substantially similar to the terms of this Agreement.

Section 3.3   Proprietary Information. Nothing contained in this Agreement shall convey any rights, title, interest or ownership to Service Provider of any of Producer's intellectual property or any intellectual property provided by a third party to Producer. Further, Service Provider shall not display or use for advertising purposes any material developed under this Agreement without the express prior written consent of Producer. Such consent may be withheld in Producer's sole discretion.

Section 3.4   Confidential Information. During the Term, the Parties may become privy to non-public confidential or proprietary information of the other Party with respect to such other Party's business, products, research and development, services, contracts (including with third parties and this Agreement), and its clients, customers, independent contractors, employees, suppliers and other business relations, including information concerning such other Party's intellectual property rights, business and management methods and techniques, market information and analysis, financial reports and statements, instruction manuals, know-how, strategic plans, technology and trade secrets, and with respect to Producer, its clients' products, services, marketing campaigns and events (collectively, "<u>Confidential Information</u>"). All Work Product (as defined herein) is deemed to be Confidential Information of Producer. During the Term and thereafter, neither party shall (and each Party shall cause its Affiliates, agents, employees, subcontractors and representatives not to) disclose, divulge, use or make available any of the Confidential Information of the other Party to any entity or person (a) without the other Party's prior written consent, or (b) in connection with any activity or business other than that of the other Party; provided, however, that this provision shall not apply to information that (i) is part of the public domain; (ii) was demonstrably in the possession of the receiving Party prior to its disclosure; (iii) is hereafter acquired by the receiving Party through a third party under no obligation of confidence, (iv) is independently developed by the receiving Party without the benefit or use of the other Party's information as evidenced by such receiving Party's written records, or (v) which is required to be disclosed by law or court order. Service Provider and Service Provider's Affiliates, agents, employees, subcontractors or representatives shall not, without the prior written consent of Producer in each instance, make any public announcement (including any online announcement or social media post) which identifies, relates to, or otherwise gives publicity to Producer, Producer's clients or this Agreement.

<u>Section 3.5</u> <u>Ownership</u>. Except for pre-existing intellectual property owned by Service Provider, as evidenced by

Service Provider's written records, Producer shall own all right, title, and interest in and to all work product that is conceived, written or created by Service Provider's employees, alone or jointly with third parties, in connection with this Agreement ("<u>Work Product</u>"). Service Provider agrees to assign to Producer all inventions, copyrights, patents, trade secrets, and other proprietary rights therein (including renewals thereof) ("<u>Intellectual Property Rights</u>") developed in the performance of the Services, except as otherwise set forth in this Agreement. Service Provider agrees to provide all assistance reasonably requested by Producer, both during and subsequent to the Term of this Agreement, in the establishment, preservation and enforcement of Producer's rights in the Work Product and Intellectual Property Rights. Service Provider acknowledges and agrees that Service Provider shall not use any video, photograph or other material, media or otherwise, created by Service Provider for Producer without the prior express written consent of Producer. Such consent may be withheld in Producer's sole discretion.

Section 3.6   <u>Name and Likeness; Release and Waiver</u>. Service Provider hereby grants to Producer and to its licensees, assignees and other successors in interest the right to film, videotape, photograph, record, digitize or otherwise reproduce Service Provider and any or all of Service Provider's employees and subcontractors in connection with the Event ("<u>Reproduction Rights</u>") and further grants all rights of every kind and character whatsoever royalty free, worldwide and in perpetuity in and to all photographs and video or audio recordings resulting from Producer's Reproduction Rights ("<u>Materials</u>"). Service Provider authorizes Producer to use and license others to use the Materials in any manner or media whatsoever, including without limitation, in any audio only or audiovisual work, in any digital online media, social media, or print media, for on-line streaming, on broadcast and digital radio, on television and in feature or documentary films (collectively, "Content") as well as use Service Provider's name and the names of its employees and subcontractors. Service Provider acknowledges that Producer shall be the owner of all rights of any kind, including copyright in and to the Materials and Content. Service Provider hereby waives any right that Service Provider may have to inspect or approve the Materials or the Contents as well as any publication of them, including without limitation, any claims for libel or violation of any right of publicity or privacy. Service Provider shall obtain a written grant, waiver and release from any and all of Service Provider's employees and approved subcontractors consisting of the same terms as set forth in this Section 3.6.

Section 3.7   Non-Solicitation. For the duration of this Agreement and for one (1) year from date of termination of this Agreement, Service Provider will not directly or indirectly solicit, for Service Provider's competitive business purpose, those clients and customers of Producer that are not currently or within the year prior to execution of this Agreement engaged in business with Service Provider.

ARTICLE IV: INDEMNIFICATION; INSURANCE; LIABILITY

Section 4.1   Indemnification. Service Provider shall and hereby agrees to indemnify, defend, reimburse, and hold harmless Producer and its respective clients, Affiliates, agents, employees, directors, officers and representatives (each, an "Indemnitee"), from and against any and all claims, demands (whether rightful or baseless), liabilities, losses, damages, injuries (including death), actions, causes of action, suits, proceedings, judgments and expenses, including reasonable attorneys' fees and court costs (collectively, "Claims"), arising out of or related to: (a) any breach by Service Provider of any provision hereof or the inaccuracy of any warranty or representation made by Service Provider in this Agreement; (b) any Claims from Service Provider's Affiliates, agents, employees, directors, subcontractors or representatives arising out of or related to the Services, including, without limitation, Service Provider's failure to pay; (c) any act or omission to act by Service Provider or Service Provider's Affiliates, agents, employees, directors, subcontractors or representatives related to the performance of this Agreement; or (d) the Services. Within five (5) business days after receipt of such notice of any Claim, Service Provider shall undertake the defense of each such Claim with counsel reasonably satisfactory to and approved by Producer. If Service Provider fails to undertake and sustain the defense of any Claim in the manner required by this Agreement, Producer may engage separate counsel, pay, settle, or otherwise finally resolve such Claim for the account and at the risk and expense of Service Provider. Service Provider may not settle any Claim without the prior written consent of Producer. If Service Provider undertakes the defense of a Claim in the manner required by this Section 4.1, Producer may, at its own expense, engage separate counsel and participate in the defense of any Claim brought against it.

Section 4.2   Insurance. During the Term, Service Provider and any approved subcontractors, as applicable, shall maintain the insurance coverage described in Exhibit B attached hereto.

Section 4.3   Limitation of Liability. IN NO EVENT SHALL PRODUCER BE LIABLE FOR ANY INCIDENTAL, INDIRECT, PUNITIVE, SPECIAL OR CONSEQUENTIAL DAMAGES FOR ANY CLAIM (INCLUDING PRODUCER'S NEGLIGENCE) ARISING OUT OF THIS AGREEMENT, REGARDLESS OF THE CAUSE OF ACTION AND EVEN

IF A PARTY HAS BEEN ADVISED OF THE POSSIBILITY OF SUCH DAMAGES.

ARTICLE V: REPRESENTATIONS AND WARRANTIES

Section 5.1   Representations and Warranties. Each Party represents and warrants to the other Party that (a) it has the full power and authority to enter into this Agreement, (b) the execution, delivery and performance of this Agreement has been duly authorized and constitutes a valid and binding agreement of such Party, and (c) the execution, delivery and performance of this Agreement shall not result in the breach of, or constitute a default under, or violate any provision of, any agreement or other instrument to which such Party is a party. Service Provider represents and warrants that (a) it is authorized to perform the Services and the Services shall be performed in a professional, timely, diligent, and workmanlike manner in accordance with recognized industry standards and in accordance with all applicable laws, rules or regulations, (b) Service Provider and each of its agents, employees, subcontractors or representatives satisfy all of the training, certification and/or licensing requirements for the jurisdiction in which the Services are being provided, and (c) Service Provider's performance of the Services shall not infringe upon the intellectual property rights of any third party.

ARTICLE VI: MISCELLANEOUS

Section 6.1   Affiliate. "Affiliate" means any entity or individual that, directly or indirectly through one or more intermediaries, controls, is controlled by, or is under common control with, the specified entity or individual. As used in this definition of Affiliate, "control" means the possession, directly or indirectly, of the power to direct or cause the direction of the management and policies of an entity or individual, whether through ownership of voting securities, by contract or otherwise.

Section 6.2   Notices. All demands, documents, notices, payments, reports, requests, returns or other communications ("Notices") delivered pursuant to the conditions, provisions and terms contained in this Agreement and other applicable law will be in writing and will be deemed to be sufficient if (a) delivered personally, (b) mailed by registered or certified mail, return receipt requested, postage prepaid, (c) sent by facsimile or other electronic transmission device, or (d) sent by a nationally-recognized, overnight courier, to the Parties at their respective addresses contained in this Agreement. All such Notices will be deemed to have been delivered and received (a) in the case of personal delivery, on the date of such delivery, (b) in the case of delivery by certified or registered mail, on the third (3rd) business day following such mailing, (c) in the case of delivery by facsimile or other electronic transmission device, on the date of such delivery if delivered on a business day, or if not delivered on a business day, then on the next business day after the day delivered, and (d) in the case of delivery by a nationally-recognized, overnight courier guaranteeing next business day delivery, on the business day following dispatch.

Section 6.3   Independent Contractor. Service Provider's engagement and provision of the Services shall be as an independent contractor to Producer, and neither Service Provider nor any of its Affiliates, agents, employees, directors, subcontractors or representatives shall be an employee, joint venturer or partner of Producer for any reason. As an independent contractor to Producer, Service Provider shall be solely responsible for all federal, local, provincial and state employment (including self-employment), income, social security and other similar levies and taxes payable by Service Provider on or with respect to its receipt of the Fees.

Section 6.4 <u>Assignment; Further Assurances</u>. This Agreement may not be assigned by Service Provider without the prior written consent of Producer. Each of the Parties shall execute any other documents and take any other actions as may be reasonably necessary to carry out the intent and purpose of this Agreement.

Section 6.5 <u>Time of Essence</u>. Time is of the essence in the performance of the Services in connection with this Agreement.

Section 6.6 <u>Waivers; Severability</u>. No failure or delay by any Party in exercising any right, power or privilege under this Agreement shall operate as a waiver thereof nor shall any single or partial exercise of any right, power or privilege hereunder preclude any other or further exercise thereof or the exercise of any other right, power or privilege. In the event that any part of this Agreement shall be declared unenforceable or invalid, the remaining parts shall continue to be valid and enforceable.

Section 6.7 <u>Attorneys' Fees</u>. In the event of a dispute arising under or related to this Agreement, whether or not a lawsuit or other proceeding is filed, the prevailing party shall be entitled to recover its attorneys' fees and costs, including attorneys' fees and costs incurred in litigating entitlement to attorneys' fees and costs.

Section 6.8 <u>Governing Law and Venue; Waiver of Jury Trial</u>. The execution, validity, interpretation and performance of this Agreement shall be governed by [MUST SET OUT WHAT STATE OR PROVINCE LAW APPLIES] law. Each of the Parties irrevocably and unconditionally submits to the exclusive jurisdiction and venue of any [NAME OF STATE] state court or United States federal court sitting in or having jurisdiction over [NAME OF CITY WHERE THE

COURT IS LOCATED] and any appellate court from any such state court or federal court, in any proceeding arising out of or related to this Agreement.

Section 6.9   Counterparts; Entire Agreement. This Agreement may be executed by facsimile, e-signature, or pdf/email and/or in counterparts and any such execution shall be a valid and binding execution hereof. This Agreement (including the Exhibits attached hereto) embodies the entire agreement and understanding of the Parties hereto, and supersedes all prior or contemporaneous written or oral communications or agreements between Producer and Service Provider, regarding the subject matter hereof. This Agreement may only be amended by written agreement between Producer and Service Provider.

IN WITNESS WHEREOF, the Parties executed this Agreement as of the Effective Date.

Producer:

Signature:____

Name and Title: _____

SERVICE PROVIDER: *(Service Provider Legal Entity or Individual Name)*

Signature:____

Name and Title: _____

EXHIBIT A

Services

During the Term, Service Provider will provide the following Services in accordance with the following schedule:

Fees

In exchange for Service Provider's provision of the Services, Producer agrees to pay Service Provider $[_____], which is inclusive of all taxes, costs and expenses arising out of the Services (the "<u>Fees</u>"). Service Provider will invoice Producer for the Fees and Producer will pay for the Fees in accordance with the provisions of the Agreement.

EXHIBIT B

Service Provider Insurance Requirements

CHAPTER 4

SOCIAL MEDIA INFLUENCER AGREEMENT

Social Media Influencer Agreement Chapter Notes

Using well known social media influencers has become a very effective way for companies to connect with large and engaged audiences. It is essential that both a company and the influencer outlines each other's expectations in an influencer agreement.

Key factors such as, schedules, types of content required, payments, Federal Trade Commission rules and usage rights are necessary to define and clarify so that the relationship between the company and influencer are mutually beneficial.

Social media influencer agreements need to be tailored according to the type of work or campaign required by a company. An influencer agreement for a YouTube influencer may be different from that of an Instagram influencer or blogger. In order to align each party's expectations, the influencer agreement should contain the following points.

1. The key to the agreement is to be very clear what services the influencer is providing. The agreement should include each specific service being provided or list services in a scope of work document attached to the main agreement. Specific deliverables should be stated.

2. Standards- A company may require the influencer to follow certain style and creative guidelines that a company has. The influencer will also have to abide by certain disclosures that are mandatory under the Federal Trade Commission Endorsement Guidelines. Essentially any influencer who does

an endorsement or testimonial needs to disclose that they are being paid for their services or being provided with free products.

3. Deadlines- It is essential to be specific about when certain deliverables need to be provided by the influencer. If a company is working on a campaign then it is important that the influencer is aligned with their schedule and provides timely and relevant posts, tweets or videos that are part of or can be incorporated in the brand's campaign.

4. Non-Disparagement- A company will want to ensure that an influencer does not do or say anything that could affect their brand or a product.

5. Compensation- The agreement should state exactly what for and when the influencer is getting paid. Is it a per post or per tweet payment or a fixed payment for numerous posts, tweets and videos? This will depend on what the company needs from the influencer and how it fits within their campaign.

6. Term- If a company is using an influencer for a specific campaign or product launch they will need to agree how long their services are needed and whether a period of exclusivity is needed. In some cases, a brand will ask that the influencer does not mention a competitor's product for a certain period after the end of their engagement. A clear start and end date is essential.

7. Ownership- The brand and the influencer will need to agree on ownership of the content, copyrights, licenses and clearances for third party use of content.

In most cases the brand will ask for full ownership of the content created by the influencer.

8. Creative Control- Most influencers will ask for creative control over the content they create for a brand. Well known influencers are hired by brands to reach their audience so most will insist on no creative interference from a brand.

SOCIAL MEDIA INFLUENCER AGREEMENT

This Influencer Agreement ("Agreement") is entered into by and between [NAME OF INFLUENCER] ("Influencer") and [NAME OF PRODUCTION COMPANY] ("PRODUCER"), for the benefit of its clients (each, an "Advertiser" and collectively, "Advertisers"). This Agreement will be effective as of the date set forth below (the "Effective Date").

In consideration of the mutual agreements contained herein and for other good and valuable consideration, the receipt and sufficiency of which are hereby acknowledged, the parties hereto, intending to be legally bound, hereby agree as follows:

I. Influencer Services.

    a. Scope. Subject to the terms of the Agreement, Influencer shall provide the Services described in each Statement of Work ("SOW") attached or entered into by the parties pursuant to the Agreement, and provide and publish all of the content set forth therein ("Influencer Content").

    b. Standards. Influencer shall perform its Services and provide all Influencer Content hereunder in accordance with any general creative, editorial, aesthetic and technical requirements, design features and other guidelines and specifications provided herein, in the applicable SOW, or otherwise communicated by PRODUCER or any Advertiser (collectively, the "Specifications"), as well as in compliance with all applicable federal, foreign, international, state/provincial/territorial, local or other laws, rules or regulations, and self-regulatory guidelines (collectively, "Laws"), including without limitation, the

Federal Trade Commission's Guidelines on Endorsements and Testimonials and PRODUCER's Influencer Guidelines, attached as Exhibit A.

    c. <u>Deadlines.</u> Influencer shall provide the Services and complete and deliver the Influencer Content according to the deadlines set forth in the applicable SOW. The parties hereto acknowledge and agree that time is of the essence of this Agreement

    d. <u>Right to Monitor</u>. PRODUCER reserves the right, but does not have an obligation, to monitor and/or review all Influencer Content. PRODUCER reserves the right at all times to require Influencer to edit, take down, or otherwise remove Influencer Content published through its social media accounts that in PRODUCER's sole discretion are objectionable or in violation of this Agreement or the Influencer Guidelines.

    e. <u>No Disparaging Impact</u>. Influencer acknowledges that the reputation of PRODUCER and of each Advertiser and its products and services is of the highest order. In no event shall Influencer, in the performance of the Services or otherwise during the Term, take any action that adversely affects Advertiser, PRODUCER or any of their parents, affiliated and/or subsidiary companies, and/or their respective image, brand, reputation, products and/or services, or that casts any of the foregoing in a negative or disparaging or light, as determined by PRODUCER and/or Advertiser, in their respective sole and absolute discretion, as applicable. In particular, Influencer shall ensure that, at all times during the Term hereof, Influencer's conduct shall reflect adherence to the highest professional, moral and ethical standards. If, in the absolute judgment of PRODUCER and/or the applicable Advertiser, any act or omission of Influencer is inconsistent with any of the foregoing, PRODUCER may immediately terminate this Agreement for cause. PRODUCER's and/or Advertiser's decision on all matters arising under this paragraph shall be conclusive, and its rights under this paragraph shall be in addition to any other rights or remedies, which PRODUCER and/or Advertiser may have hereunder or at law or in equity.

    f. Independent Contractor. The relationship of Influencer to PRODUCER shall be that of an independent contractor rendering professional services. Influencer shall not have any authority to execute contracts or make commitments on behalf of PRODUCER (or Advertiser). Nothing contained herein shall be deemed to create the relationship of employer/employee, principal/agent, joint venturer or partner between Influencer and PRODUCER (or Advertiser). Further, Influencer recognizes that in view of its status as an independent contractor, neither it nor its employees, contractors, representatives or agents will be entitled to participate in or receive any fringe benefits normally granted to PRODUCER's employees under such programs, including, but not limited to, worker's compensation, voluntary disability, travel accident insurance, medical/dental insurance, life insurance, long-term disability, holiday pay, sick pay, salary continuation pay, leaves of absence (paid or unpaid), pension plan and savings plan. Influencer shall be responsible for and shall defend, indemnify and hold harmless PRODUCER against any and all Damages (as defined below) in connection with Influencer's engagement as an independent contractor.

II. Compensation; Taxes.

    a. Compensation. In consideration for Influencer's full performance of all Services, provision of Influencer Content, and the grant of all rights granted by Influencer hereunder, and subject to all terms and conditions hereof, Influencer shall be entitled to receive the compensation in the manner, at the rates and at the times indicated in the applicable SOW (collectively, the "Compensation"). Influencer hereby acknowledges and agrees that the Compensation shall cover all of the Services, Influencer Content, and all fees, hourly rates, costs and/or expenses incurred by Influencer in connection therewith and with this Agreement. Unless otherwise expressly provided herein, Influencer shall be responsible for paying all costs and expenses required in connection with the full performance of the Services and full delivery of the Influencer Content. In no event shall PRODUCER be required to pay any compensation to Influencer in excess of the Compensation.

b. Taxes. Influencer agrees and acknowledges that taxes or other amounts will not be withheld from any Compensation or other amounts payable to Influencer hereunder. Influencer agrees and acknowledges that it has sole responsibility and liability for any and all taxes, contributions, penalties, interest or other sums arising out of the Compensation and/or any other amounts and/or expenses paid pursuant to this Agreement, the understanding being that the quoted rates include therein a component attributable to such amounts.

III. Term.

a. Term. This Agreement will remain in effect from the Effective Date until it is terminated by either party as provided below (the "Term"). The term of each SOW will be as set forth in such SOW.

b. Termination of Agreement Without Cause. PRODUCER may immediately terminate this Agreement (or any individual Influencer Content hereunder) at any time, without cause, by giving written notice to Influencer. In the event that PRODUCER terminates this Agreement without cause as set forth above, Influencer shall be entitled to any installment of the Compensation owing but not yet paid to Influencer in accordance with the applicable SOW as of the date of such termination (and any portion of any installment paid to Influencer that is more than what Influencer is entitled to as of the date of termination shall be immediately refunded to PRODUCER).

c. Termination by Parties for Cause. Either party may terminate this Agreement (i) upon ten (10) days prior written notice to the other party in the event such other party breaches this Agreement and fails to cure such breach within such ten (10) day notice period, or (i) immediately upon written notice to the other party in the event such other party becomes insolvent, files a petition for bankruptcy, executes an assignment for the benefit of creditors or takes advantage of any insolvency or any other like statute. In the event of termination by PRODUCER under subsection (i), Influencer will promptly refund a pro-rata portion of Compensation received as of the date of termination.

d. Surviving Provisions. Sections IV - X hereof (and those terms in the applicable SOW, which by their nature ought to survive) shall survive the expiration or early termination of this Agreement.

IV. Likeness.

a. Right to Use Likeness. Influencer hereby grants PRODUCER, Advertiser(s), and its/their designees, a royalty-free, perpetual, worldwide license and right to photograph, record, publish, display, exploit, modify, edit, reproduce and otherwise use Influencer's name, image, likeness, voice, performance, social media handles, nicknames, biographical materials, statements, testimonials, and other indicia, and any portion thereof (collectively, "Likeness"), in any and all media (now or hereafter known) for any and all purposes in connection with (a) the advertising and/or promotion of Advertiser's products or services, (b) posting, publication and/or any other exploitation of any of the Influencer Content, (c) any personal appearances of Influencer and/or any recordings thereof, and/or (d) the advertising, promotion, marketing, selling, and/or development of PRODUCER, without in each and every instance any additional permissions from and/or compensation or notices to Influencer. All advertising, promotional and/or publicity materials produced by or on behalf of PRODUCER and/or Advertiser shall be and remain the sole and absolute property of PRODUCER (and/or Advertiser, as the case may be), and the Influencer will not have any right, title or interest of any kind in or to said materials, or any component part, element or reproduction thereof. Influencer hereby waives any moral rights and any other similar rights he or she may have in such advertising, promotional and/or publicity materials.

b. <u>No Guild or Other Obligations</u>. Influencer hereby represents and warrants that Influencer is not a member of any guild, union or similar organization such that the use of such Influencer's name, likeness, voice, performance, biographical materials, statements or testimonials as contemplated hereunder would trigger any guild, union or third party payments or other obligations. In the event this status changes, Influencer will immediately notify PRODUCER and/or Advertiser.

V. Grant of Rights and Use of Materials. Influencer hereby grants to PRODUCER, for itself and for the benefit of Advertiser, a fully paid up and royalty free, perpetual and irrevocable, non- exclusive worldwide unlimited right and license to use, publicly display, distribute, sub-license, modify, and otherwise exploit, in any and all media, channel, platform, or format now known or hereafter developed, in whole or in part, Influencer's Likeness and any and all Influencer Content created under this Agreement, without further notice, approval or compensation to Influencer or any third party. PRODUCER and Advertiser will have the right to authorize others to exercise any and/or all of the rights granted to PRODUCER under this Agreement, whether by license, sublicense, assignment or otherwise.

VI. Ownership

a. Influencer Content. For any Influencer Content created hereunder, including, without limitation, all social media posts authored by Influencer, Influencer acknowledges that he/she has no right, title or interest (and agree that he/she will not claim any right, title, or interest) in or to any such Influencer Content, and Influencer further acknowledges and agrees that PRODUCER and/or Advertiser shall own all rights, title and interest in or to all such Influencer Content. For the avoidance of doubt, and to further evidence the full ownership of the Influencer Content by PRODUCER, Influencer hereby assigns to PRODUCER all rights, title and interest to the Influencer Content. Influencer agrees to assist PRODUCER and/or Advertiser in the enforcement of its proprietary rights over all such Influencer Content, including the prompt execution of any additional documents that may be reasonably requested by PRODUCER and/or Advertiser. If Influencer fails to cooperate with or assist, execute, acknowledge, verify or deliver any such document requested by PRODUCER and/or Advertiser, Influencer hereby irrevocably appoints PRODUCER and/or Advertiser (as applicable) and its authorized officers and agents as Influencer's agent and attorney-in-fact to act in Influencer's place to execute, acknowledge, verify, and/or deliver any such document (as applicable) on Influencer's behalf. To the fullest extent allowable under any applicable law, you hereby irrevocably waive or assign to PRODUCER the benefits of any provision of law known as "droit moral," "moral rights" or any similar rights or principles of law in any country of the world which you may now or later have in the Influencer Content, and agree not to institute or permit any action or lawsuit on the ground that the Influencer Content or any other materials or content based upon the Influencer Content constitutes an infringement of your droit moral or is in any way a defamation or mutilation of the Influencer Content or any part thereof, or contains unauthorized variations, alterations, modifications, changes or translations.

b. <u>Advertiser Marks</u>. Influencer agrees that any trademarks, trade names, logos, service marks and/or other indicia of Advertiser and/or its parent, affiliated and/or subsidiary companies (collectively, the "Advertiser Marks") and any materials provided to Influencer by or on behalf of Advertiser (and/or any of its parent, affiliated and/or subsidiary companies and/or their respective employees, representatives, contractors or agents) hereunder shall be owned exclusively by and shall inure solely to the benefit of Advertiser. Influencer further agrees that it will not claim any right in or to the Advertiser Marks and/or such materials. Influencer shall not use or modify any Advertiser Marks or such materials without the prior written approval of PRODUCER and/or Advertiser in each instance.

c. <u>PRODUCER Marks</u>. Influencer agrees that any trademarks, trade names, logos, service marks and/or other indicia of PRODUCER and/or its parent, affiliated and/or subsidiary companies (collectively, the "PRODUCER Marks") and any materials provided to Influencer by or on behalf of PRODUCER (and/or any of its parent, affiliated and/or subsidiary companies and/or their respective employees, representatives, contractors or agents) hereunder shall be owned exclusively by and shall inure solely to the benefit of PRODUCER. Influencer further agrees that it will not claim any right in or to the PRODUCER Marks and/ or such materials. Influencer shall not use or modify any PRODUCER Marks or such materials without the prior written approval of PRODUCER in each instance.

VII. Influencer Representations and Warranties. Influencer represents, warrants and covenants to PRODUCER that:

a. Influencer has the full right, power and authority to enter into this Agreement, grant the rights granted herein, and fully perform its obligations hereunder, and, in particular, Influencer is not subject to any obligation or disability that will or might hinder or prevent the full completion and performance by Influencer of all obligations and conditions hereunder. Influencer has reached the age of majority in his or her jurisdiction and is a legal resident of (i) Canada, or (ii) the fifty (50) United States or the District of Columbia.

b. Except as otherwise specifically authorized in writing by PRODUCER, the Influencer Content is wholly original with Influencer, and PRODUCER's or Advertiser's use thereof does not and will not infringe any patents, copyrights, trademarks, trade secrets or other intellectual property rights or violate the right of privacy, publicity or other rights of any third party, nor has any claim of such infringement or violation been threatened or asserted against Influencer or others.

c. The Influencer Content and Influencer's performance of the Services and all of its other obligations under this

Agreement will comply with the Specifications and all other terms and conditions of this Agreement.

d. The Influencer Content (a) is not false and/or defamatory, inaccurate, libelous, abusive, vulgar, hateful, harassing or threatening, obscene, offensive, or contain disparaging remarks about other people or companies; (b) does not endorse any form of hate or hate group; (c) is not profane or pornographic; (d) is not sexually oriented, explicit or suggestive; (e) is not unnecessarily violent nor derogatory of any ethnic, racial, gender, religious, professional or age group; (f) does not promote alcohol, illegal drugs, tobacco, firearms/weapons (or the use of any of the foregoing); (g) does not promote any activities that may be construed as unsafe or dangerous; (h) is in compliance with all applicable Law; or (i) unless specifically approved by PRODUCER, does not promote any particular political agenda or message.

e. All testimonials or other similar statements by Influencer shall be expressions of his/her personal experience and belief, and shall be valid unless and until he/she advises PRODUCER in writing otherwise.

VIII. Confidentiality.

a. Definition of Confidential Information. For purposes of this Agreement, the term "Confidential Information" shall be deemed to include all information and materials furnished by or on behalf of any of PRODUCER and/or Advertiser to Influencer, and/or otherwise arising from and/or in connection with the Services.

b. Ownership and Non-Disclosure of Confidential Information. Influencer agrees and acknowledges that he or she shall have no proprietary interest in any of the Confidential Information, and will not disclose, communicate or publish the nature or content of such Confidential Information to any person or entity, nor use, except as authorized in writing by PRODUCER and/or Advertiser, any of the Confidential Information that Influencer receives, acquires or obtains in connection with this Agreement. In the event the Influencer becomes legally compelled to disclose any of the Confidential Information, Influencer shall provide PRODUCER with prompt notice thereof and shall not divulge any information until PRODUCER and/or Advertiser (or their designees) has had the opportunity to seek a protective order or other appropriate remedy to curtail such disclosure. If such actions are unsuccessful, or PRODUCER and/or Advertiser (or their designees) otherwise waives the right to seek such remedies, Influencer shall disclose only that portion of the Confidential Information which it is legally required to disclose. Influencer shall not issue or authorize publication of any news story or publicity relating to Influencer's Services and/or any rights hereunder, unless in each instance approved in advance and in writing by PRODUCER and/or Advertiser (at their sole discretion).

c. Remedies. The parties acknowledge and agree that remedy at law for a breach or threatened breach of any of the provisions under this Section VIII would be inadequate. In recognition of this fact, and without limiting any other rights or remedies available to PRODUCER or Advertiser hereunder, in the event of a breach or threatened breach by the Influencer of any of the provisions contained in this Section VII, PRODUCER and/or Advertiser shall be entitled to obtain provisional equitable relief in the form of temporary restraining order and/or temporary injunction or any other provisional equitable remedy which may then be available, and Influencer hereby agrees not to contest same.

IX. **Indemnification**. Influencer shall defend, indemnify and hold PRODUCER and Advertiser, and their respective parent, subsidiary and affiliated companies, including without limitation, any licensee of any subsidiary, and their respective officers, directors, agents, and employees (collectively, "Indemnified Parties") harmless from and against any and all costs, liabilities, demands, claims, suits, actions, damages, losses, judgments and expenses, including without limitation, attorneys' fees (collectively, "Damages") arising out of or related to: (a) any breach or alleged breach of this Agreement by Influencer; and/or (b) Influencer's Services or the Influencer Content. PRODUCER and/or Advertiser may, at its election, assume the defense, settlement or other resolution of such claim with counsel of its own choosing, at Influencer's cost and expense.

X. **Miscellaneous**.

a. <u>Third Party Beneficiary</u>. The parties hereto hereby acknowledge and agree that all Advertisers identified in any applicable SOW are each an intended third party beneficiary of this Agreement. In furtherance of, but without limiting the foregoing, all benefits and rights licensed, assigned, or otherwise granted to PRODUCER hereunder are granted for the benefit of the Advertiser listed in the applicable SOW, and Advertiser shall have the full right and authority to enjoy all such benefits and exercise all such rights. b. <u>Services Unique</u>. It is expressly understood and agreed that the Services and the rights and privileges granted to PRODUCER and Advertiser hereunder are of a special, unique, unusual, extraordinary, and intellectual character, giving them a peculiar value the loss of which cannot be reasonably or adequately compensated in damages in an action at law, and that Influencer's failure or refusal to perform its obligations hereunder would cause irreparable harm or damage to PRODUCER and

Advertiser. Should Influencer fail or refuse to perform such obligations, PRODUCER shall be entitled to seek injunctive or other equitable relief against Influencer to prevent the continuance of such failure or refusal or to prevent Influencer from performing services for or granting rights to others in violation of this Agreement.

c. Assignment. This Agreement may not be assigned by the Influencer, or any of the Influencer's duties hereunder delegated to any other person or entity, without the prior written consent of the PRODUCER, and any such purported assignment or delegation shall be null and void ab initio.

d. Further Assurances. Each of the parties agrees to execute such further documents and other instruments and perform such further acts as may be reasonably required or desirable to carry out the provisions hereof and the transactions contemplated hereby.

e. Binding Effect. This Agreement shall be binding upon, shall inure to the benefit of, and shall be enforceable by PRODUCER, the Advertiser, the Influencer and their respective permitted successors and assigns. Nothing expressed or implied herein is intended to confer upon any person, other than the Advertiser, PRODUCER, the Influencer and their respective permitted successors and assigns, any rights, remedies, obligations or liabilities under or by reason of this Agreement.

f. Severability. If any provision of this Agreement is determined by a court of competent jurisdiction to be unenforceable or invalid, that provision shall be limited or eliminated to the minimum extent necessary so that this Agreement shall otherwise remain in full force and effect and the other provisions hereof shall be unaffected.

g. <u>Entire Agreement</u>. This Agreement, together with the applicable Statements of Work, is intended to embody the final, complete and exclusive agreement among the parties with respect to the subject matter hereof and supersedes all prior agreements, understandings and representations, whether written or oral, with respect thereto, and may not be contradicted by evidence of any prior or contemporaneous agreement, understanding or representation, whether written or oral.

h. <u>Amendment, Modification and Waiver</u>. This Agreement may not be amended or modified or any provision hereof or obligation arising hereunder waived except in a writing signed by the party against which enforcement is sought.

i. <u>Governing Law</u>. Except as otherwise prohibited by law, this Agreement shall be governed by and construed in accordance with the laws of the State of [NAME OF STATE] without regard to its conflicts of laws principles.

j. <u>Dispute Resolution and Venue</u>. Any dispute arising out of or relating to this Agreement shall be brought exclusively in state or federal courts sitting [NAME OF STATE], with the parties hereto waiving any claim or defense that such forum is inconvenient or improper. Each party agrees that such court shall have jurisdiction over such party, consents to service of process in any manner authorized by [NEED TO DEFINE WHAT STATE LAW APPLIES], and agrees that a final judgment in any such action or proceeding shall be conclusive and may be enforced in other jurisdictions by suit on the judgment or in any other manner specified by law. If either party shall bring an action against the other by reason of any alleged breach of any covenant or provision hereof, or otherwise arising out of or relating to this Agreement, the unsuccessful party shall pay to the prevailing party all reasonable attorneys' fees and costs actually incurred by the prevailing party, in addition to any other relief to which such party may be entitled.

    k. <u>Interpretation</u>. The section headings of this Agreement are for convenience of reference only and shall not be deemed to alter or affect any provision hereof. The language in all parts of this Agreement shall be construed simply, in accordance with its fair meaning, and not strictly for or against either of the parties hereto. Where applicable, words appearing in the singular shall include the plural, the word "including" shall be deemed to mean "including, without limitation," and words such as "hereof," "hereunder" and similar terms shall be deemed to refer to this Agreement as a whole. Without limiting the foregoing, there shall be no presumption against either party on the grounds that such party was responsible for drafting this Agreement or any provision hereof.

    l. <u>Counterparts</u>. This Agreement may be executed in original, facsimile or other electronic counterparts, each of which shall be deemed an original and all of which together shall constitute one instrument.

IN WITNESS WHEREOF, the parties have caused this Agreement to be executed by their respective duly authorized representatives as of the Effective Date.

Influencer: PRODUCER:

                                  Name:

                                  Title:

                                  Date:

EXHIBIT A: Influencer Guidelines

These Influencer Guidelines ("Guidelines") outline your disclosure responsibilities and best practices by which you must abide when providing and posting Influencer Content, including online content and commentary, in connection with the Influencer Agreement. You must comply with these Guidelines at all times, so please read this document carefully.

General Considerations

You are personally and legally responsible for your statements and compliance with applicable laws, rules, regulations and industry guidelines, including the Federal Trade Commission Guides Concerning the Use of Endorsements and Testimonials in Advertising, 16 CFR Part 255 (the "FTC Guides").

Exercise caution and appropriate restraint with regard to conclusions, exaggeration, colorful language, speculation, obscenity, the materials you use, images and/or video that you may post, and derogatory remarks or characterizations.

Limit your posting of content related to an Advertiser to those websites and channels as approved by PRODUCER or the

Advertiser.

Who You Are

Identify yourself as the "official" author of the posting in an obvious, clear position on the page.

Don't impersonate or imply that you are any other person or entity, including an employee of PRODUCER or Advertiser.

Clearly state that your views and comments are solely your own and do not represent those of Advertiser. For example, an acceptable disclosure would be: "This blog post was sponsored by Nike but the opinions are all my own."

Your Relationship to Advertiser

When posting comments or content about Advertiser or any of its products, you must **clearly and conspicuously** disclose the nature of your connection to Advertiser. This includes:

- o If you have been provided with free products from Advertiser to comment on or review,

- o If you are a paid endorser of an Advertiser's product or are being compensated in any way by Advertiser; or

- o If you are receiving any other benefits or incentives from Advertiser.

These disclosures should be **prominent, easily understandable,** and **in close physical proximity** to any comments by you related to Advertiser or its products.

- o Include the disclosure within each post itself (an endorsement in one tweet followed by disclosure in a second tweet, or a disclosure on a separate page is *not* enough).

o The form/medium of the disclosure should match the form/medium of the content (e.g., if the post is a video, the disclosure should be provided in the video).

o Tag posts or tweets **#sponsored**, **#paid**, or **#ad** (but don't use the abbreviation **#spon** or put the hashtags directly after a link). You may also provide organic disclosures that indicate your relationship to the Advertiser (e.g. "Thanks [Advertiser] for these great samples!" or "My friends at [Advertiser] ....")

o If you need more information on how to make effective disclosures, please consult the FTC Guides[11] or Dot Com Disclosures.[22]

If you have received an item to use in connection with a giveaway, sweepstakes, contest, or other promotion that you are sponsoring, you are responsible for all elements of the promotion, including ensuring compliance with applicable laws. Do not suggest that Advertiser is affiliated with the promotion, except to state that Advertiser has provided the prize(s), if that is indeed the case. For example:

o *"This prize has been provided by Advertiser. [If Advertiser has provided any additional compensation or benefits, disclose the additional compensation/benefits; if not, say something like 'No additional compensation was*

---

1   Available at www.ftc.gov/os/2009/10/091005revisedendorsementguides.pdf
2   Available at www.ftc.gov/os/2013/03/130312dotcomdisclosures.pdf; https://www.ftc.gov/system/files/documents/plain- language/pdf-0205-endorsement-guides-faqs.pdf.

THE CONTENT MAKER'S HANDBOOK

provided.'] Advertiser is in no way sponsoring or administering this promotion [*or contest/sweepstakes/ giveaway*] and is not responsible for any operation of, or activity in connection with, the promotion."

Honesty and Accuracy

Don't make any false or unsubstantiated statements or claims about Advertiser and its prod ucts; don't comment on a product that you haven't tried.

You may only make claims about Advertiser and its products as provided by Advertiser in the Statement of Work.

Your postings, stated views, and comments must reflect your actual experience, honest opinions, findings, and beliefs and must not be misleading, deceptive, or defamatory in any way.

Be the first to correct your own mistakes, but don't alter previous posts without indicating that you have done so.

Respect

Don't make offensive comments that create an intimidating or hostile online environment, including telling lies or spreading rumors about other people, companies, products, or services.

Don't criticize or make disparaging remarks about companies or products that may be competitive with Advertiser brands and products.

Don't use ethnic or racial slurs, personal insults, obscenity, or other offensive language.

Show proper consideration for others' privacy and for topics that may be considered objectionable or inflammatory (such as politics or religion).

Don't spam others or post advertisements or other materials offering or soliciting services.

Check and respond to comments regularly, but before addressing any negative or inflammatory posts, consult with your PRODUCER contact on how to appropriately reply, deflect, address, or block the posting.

Safety

Don't post any comments or content that in any way promote unsafe activities or illegal activities or products, or that could lead to an unsafe situation involving Advertiser consumers or anyone else.

Don't post or promote materials that could harm or disrupt another person's computer or that could allow others to improperly access software or websites.

Trademarks and Other Intellectual Property

Any trademarks, logos, materials and other proprietary information that PRODUCER or Advertiser may provide to you can only be used in accordance with any guidelines provided by PRODUCER or Advertiser. Use of any other trademarks, logos, materials and other proprietary information not provided by PRODUCER or Advertiser may not be used without PRODUCER or Advertiser's prior written permission.

When posting comments or content online, respect the intellectual property and proprietary rights (including trademark, copyright, privacy, and publicity) of others. For example:

o Don't reference other brands or use any third party's trademarks, logos, or service marks unless you have all necessary permissions to do so.

o Don't cite or reference Advertiser employees, partners, suppliers or retailers that offer Advertiser branded products without PRODUCER or Advertiser's prior approval.

o Don't post or repost/republish any third-party content (e.g., photos, videos) without written permission from the person or entity that owns the content and any persons depicted or referenced in the content. An email from the author of the content is sufficient permission; permission may also be obtained through direct social messaging (DM or PM), provided you can provide a written record of the consent.

Only link to other relevant content from your post if the content on the linked site is accurate, appropriate, and not otherwise inconsistent with these Guidelines.

Proprietary and Confidential Information

Don't post confidential or proprietary information of any party.

Don't disclose personally identifiable information (such as email addresses, home street addresses, telephone numbers, or private facts), about any person.

If there is any doubt in your mind as to what is proprietary and confidential information or personally identifiable information, consult PRODUCER or Advertiser or do not post the information.

<u>Press Inquiries</u>

If a member of the media contacts you about a comment or content posting related to Advertiser, requests Advertiser information of any kind, or solicits you to make a comment related to Advertiser or your posting, please contact your PRODUCER campaign manager immediately.

Don't engage in any discussions or correspondence related to Advertiser or your online post(s) with any members of the media without first consulting your PRODUCER campaign manager.

CHAPTER 5

PERSONAL RELEASE – ALL RIGHTS

Personal Release Chapter Notes

Any content creator who is using a real person in a video that will be used for any commercial purpose will need to obtain a release. If you are filming people at a private event on private property you will need to obtain a release including people who do not speak. Some places that may seem like public venues such as a sports stadium or amusement park but are privately owned will also need releases from anyone filmed at that location.

The personal release will enable the content creator to own all rights in any footage in perpetuity. This will enable the content creator to distribute the content on any platform without any payments.

This agreement refers to the fact that the person being filmed is not a member of any union or collective bargaining agreement. This handbook does not cover any union agreements such as the Screen Actors Guild, (SAG) which has very specific rules and regulations when engaging their members. When engaging SAG members, it is essential that you engage an attorney or producer who understands the rules, regulations and payments under the most recent SAG agreement.

PERSONAL RELEASE

For good and valuable consideration, the receipt of which is hereby acknowledged, I grant to [PRODUCTION COMPANY X] ("Company") and its respective parents, affiliates, subsidiaries, licensees, successors and assigns the right and license to record, film, tape, photograph and otherwise capture, reproduce and exploit in any manner my name, stage name, voice, likeness, image, right of publicity and performance; furthermore, Company shall have the right and license to use any biographical material that I might furnish. All sound and visual recordings of any kind made of me by the Company shall be deemed "Footage."

I agree that Company shall, in perpetuity throughout the universe, (i) own all rights in and to the Footage; and (ii) have all rights necessary to exploit the Footage, in whole or in part and for any purpose, in any form of distribution including but limited to film, television, advertising and internet based distribution, now known or hereafter created in Company's sole discretion without any obligation, financial or otherwise, to me or any other third party. For purposes of illustration only, media shall include, film, television, advertising digital media, on-line media, and all other television broadcast or internet based media now known or hereafter created. Company is under no obligation to use, exhibit or exploit the Footage in any manner. I waive (i) the right to inspect or approve any use of the Footage; (ii) any rights to injunctive relief I may have in connection with this Personal Release or the use of the Footage; (iii) the right to revoke this Personal Release; and (iv) any so-called Droit Moral or "moral rights" in and to the Footage. I release and agree to hold harmless and indemnify Company, including without limitation its agents, representatives, licensees and assigns, from all claims, demands, causes of actions, damages, and other liabilities of any kind, including without limitation reasonable attorneys' fees and costs which may arise out of or in connection with the use and exploitation of the Footage. I also acknowledge that Company is not a signatory to any union or guild or other collective bargaining agreements and this Personal Release is not subject to any such union, guild or other collective bargaining agreements. I further indemnify Company and its respective employees, officers, directors, shareholders, successors, licensees, assigns and affiliated entities harmless from and against, any and all payments required by collective bargaining, guild and union agreements. I agree that no sum or other compensation of any kind, now or in the future, shall be due to me or any third party for the execution of this Personal Release and/or the use of the Footage.

This Personal Release shall be governed in accordance with the laws of the State of [NAME OF STATE], without regard for such state's principles concerning conflicts of laws or strict construction against the drafter. This Personal Release constitutes the entire agreement and understanding between the parties relating to the subject matter described herein. I shall have no right to assign this Personal Release, in whole or in part, without Company's prior written consent. I warrant that I have the right, power and authority to execute this Personal Release and grant the rights set forth herein. This Personal Release shall be binding on my representatives, heirs and permitted assigns, if any. Any claim, dispute or controversy arising out of this Personal Release, the interpretation, validity or enforceability of this Personal Release or the alleged breach thereof shall be finally and exclusively resolved by arbitration under the Rules of Arbitration of the American Arbitration Association in [NAME OF STATE], with such arbitration conducted by an arbitrator with experience in the entertainment industry. Furthermore, if a minor child is depicted in the Footage,

I represent and warrant that I am either a parent or legal guardian for such minor child and that I have complete authority to grant this Personal Release on such minor child's behalf.

AGREED TO AND ACCEPTED:

By: _____   Address:

Name: _____

Date: _____   Parent/
                                        Guardian (if
                                        applicable,
                                        circle one)

_____   Minor's Name:
                                        (if applicable)

Phone: _____   Email:

CHAPTER 6

CROWD RELEASE

Crowd Release Chapter Notes

When shooting video in a public area where people will be seen in the background it may be helpful to post a crowd release at the entrance and exit of an event or if possible on the ticket of a ticketed event on private property. This form of release can add an extra layer of protection. A large event with many people may be impossible to get a release from everyone. Having a crowd release helps to eliminate a claim by an individual in attendance. If the event is in a public area people generally give up their "reasonable right to privacy". However, if a video shoot is for commercial purposes then anyone appearing on camera and is recognizable or identifiable will need a full written release.

NOTICE: YOU MAY BE PHOTOGRAPHED AND/OR RECORDED.

By entering into this area/venue and/or attending this event, you are agreeing to be videotaped, recorded and photographed and hereby grant Anheuser-Busch and its divisions, subsidiaries, subcontractors, agencies and licensees and assigns the right (but not obligation) to use, publish, distribute and broadcast your name, likeness/image, voice or statements anywhere in the world, in any language, in print or on television, DVDs/CDs, the internet (including social networking sites), or in any other media (now known or developed later) in perpetuity.

You will not be compensated for the recording or use of your name, likeness/image, voice or statements. <u>If you do not wish to be videotaped, recorded or photographed nor have your name, likeness/image, voice or statements used in this manner, please do not enter this section.</u>

CHAPTER 7

LOCATION LICENSE AGREEMENT

Location License Agreement Chapter Notes

Content producers will need to obtain a location release from the owners of a private property where filming takes place. Without a location release a content producer runs the risk of being liable for trespass.

They will need an agreement with the property owner to ensure that they have the right to show the image of the property such as a store front or name of the company in their content.

This agreement is property owner friendly and puts numerous obligations on the producers to ensure that certain obligations and responsibilities are met.

It is essential that dates and times of the filming, including any set up, building of sets, takedown and cleanup are clearly set out in the agreement. The agreement should be clear as to how much the producers are paying for use of the location. Most location owners will ask for a damage deposit before any filming takes place.

A property owner will also list in the agreement the things that a production company can or can't do while using the location. They will also ask that the producers provide valid insurance documents listing the owners as a named insured on their policy.

This agreement sets out most of the responsibilities and obligations of both the content producer and the location owner but should be tailored to meet the specific needs of a production.

Location License Agreement

This License Agreement (the "Agreement") is made and entered into by and between [NAME OF COMPANYWITH THE LOCATION] ("Licensor") and [NAME OF PRODUCER/PRODUCTION COMPANY] ("Licensee").

1. <u>License</u>. Licensor agrees to permit Licensee to use on a non-exclusive basis, in common with Licensor and such other persons to whom Licensor may from time to time grant rights, the real property described in Schedule A attached hereto and incorporated herein for all purposes by reference (the "Property"), and Licensee accepts the right so to use the Property, upon and subject to the terms and conditions hereinafter set forth. It is hereby agreed and understood that this Agreement is merely a license to use the Property and that no right, title, estate or interest in or to the Property is granted to or vested in Licensee by virtue of this Agreement. Licensee acknowledges that all use of the Property by Licensee shall be pursuant to this Agreement and that Licensee shall not, by such use, acquire any rights in or to the Property by prescription, adverse possession or otherwise.

2. <u>Term</u>. Pursuant to Schedule D, the term of this Agreement shall be for a period of One (1) days, commencing at [TIME] AM/ PM on [DATE] (the "Commencement Date") and ending at [AM/PM] on [DATE }, unless earlier terminated as herein provided. Licensor may, by written notice to Licensee, terminate this Agreement as of the date set forth in said notice in the event that: (a)Licensee fails to pay any funds due to Licensor within two (2) days after Licensor delivers written notice to Licensee that such funds have not been paid when due; (b) Licensor reasonably believes Licensee poses a threat to the health and/or safety of

the Property, any tenants of the Property, or any of such tenants' customers or invitees, provided that Licensee shall have the right to cure such act or omission on the same day Licensor delivers written notice to Licensee that such circumstance(s) exist; (c) Licensor reasonably believes that Licensee has violated any law, statute, ordinance or recorded covenant applicable to the Property, provided that Licensee shall have the right to cure such violation within one (1) day after Licensor delivers written notice to Licensee that such circumstance(s) exists; or (d) Licensee defaults in the keeping, observance or performance of any covenant or term set forth in this Agreement (other than a default for the failure to pay any funds to Licensor that have become due and payable under this Agreement), provided that Licensee shall have the right to cure such default within one (1) day after Licensor delivers written notice to Licensee that such circumstance(s) exist. On such date as applicable in accordance with this Section 2, this Agreement shall cease and terminate and be of no further force and effect, except the provisions of Section 9 shall survive the expiration or earlier termination of this Agreement.

3. <u>Consideration</u>. Licensee shall pay to Licensor the sum or sums set forth in Schedule B attached hereto and incorporated herein for all purposes of reference. All agreed to location fees, supervisory, security, location representative, elevator operator fees, etc. shall be paid in advance prior to any equipment and/or personnel entering The Property. Payment shall be in the form of a company check or cashier's check payable to [NAME]. Notwithstanding the foregoing, the Total License Fee shall be paid by [TIME AND DATE].

4. <u>Use</u> <u>of</u> <u>Property</u>. Licensee shall use the Property for the purposes set forth in Schedule C attached hereto and incorporated herein for all purposes by reference, and shall

not use the Property for any other purpose whatsoever. Licensee shall be entering upon and occupying the Property, be deemed to have accepted the Property "AS IS", in its then condition, and Licensee hereby releases Licensor, its directors, officers, employees and agents from any liability or loss caused by any latent or patent defect therein. Licensee shall comply with all governmental rules, regulations, ordinances statutes and laws, the orders and regulations of the Insurance Services Office or any other body exercising similar functions, and all covenants, conditions and restrictions pertaining to the Property or Licensee's use thereof. Licensee shall not permit anything to be done or kept upon the Property that does or could interfere with the rights of Licensor, it's tenants or the patrons and customers of any of them, or that will annoy any of them, nor shall Licensee commit or permit any nuisance or any illegal act to be committed thereon. Licensee acknowledges that Licensor has not obtained and shall not be required to obtain authority or permission from any tenants of the Property to utilize their likeness or trade name. Licensee shall be required to obtain permission from an authorized signatory, for each and every individual tenant of the Property whose storefront, likeness or business shall be depicted in any manner or fashion. Licensee shall not be entitled or permitted to use the images or photographs of the Property in any defamatory or indecent manner as those terms are generally applied according to local and standard custom. Licensee represents, warrants and covenants that Licensor has been provided applicable script pages to be shot at the Property. Should such scenes materially change, Licensee shall provide such new script pages to Licensor whose approval shall not be unreasonably withheld. Licensee acknowledges that the public, tenants in the Property, Licensor's agents and staff, and visitors will not be restricted except during actual filming unless otherwise agreed. In the event Licensee desires to return to the Property to complete filming or add scenes or construct duplicates, Licensor shall use commercially reasonable efforts to accommodate such request upon reasonable prior notice but Licensor makes no representation, warranty or covenant that the Property will be available at any time after the time periods set forth in this Agreement. Licensee shall not store overnight equipment or vehicles unless otherwise agreed to by Licensor and, if such permission is granted, solely in strict compliance with Licensor's requirements. Parking by Licensee and any of its employees, contractors or other personnel related to Licensee's work at the Property shall be in accordance with Licensor's rules and regulations and charged at Licensor's prevailing rates, plus any and all applicable taxes.

5. Maintenance, etc. Licensee shall keep and maintain the Property in good order, condition and repair (including any such replacement and restoration required for that purpose), shall provide all precautions for safety and protection of persons and property and keep the Property free from waste. Upon termination of this Agreement, Licensee shall restore the Property to as good a condition as at the commencement of this Agreement, reasonable wear and tear accepted. Licensee agrees that Licensee shall not engage or permit at any time, any operations or activities upon, or any use or occupancy of the Property, or any portion thereof, for the purpose of or in any way involving the handling, manufacturing, treatment, storage, use, transportation, spillage, leakage, dumping, discharge or disposal (whether legal or illegal, accidental or intentional) of any hazardous substances, materials or wastes, or any wastes regulated under any local, state or federal law.

6. Improvements. Licensee shall not make any alterations, improvements or changes, nor install any fixtures, signs or billboards ("Improvements") in, upon or to the Property

without the written consent of Licensor. Any improvements made by Licensee shall, at Licensor's option, become the property of Licensor upon termination of this Agreement. Licensee shall, however, at Licensor's request, remove such improvements and repair any damage caused thereby at Licensee's sole cost and expense upon termination of this Agreement.

7. <u>Utilities</u>. During the Term, Licensee shall pay charges for water, electricity, air conditioning, gas, garbage service, telephone and all other service or utilities used upon the property.

8. <u>Insurance</u>.

>a) Licensee shall at its sole cost and expense, procure and maintain in full force and effect, insurance for the entities, in the forms, types and amounts exactly as and not less than the following: [AMOUNT OF INSURANCE COVERAGE REQUIRED]

>1) **<u>Insurance Certificate Additionally Insured:</u>**

>b) Insurance required to be maintained by Licensee hereunder shall be in companies holding a "General Policyholders' Rating" of A or better and a "financial rating" of 10 or better, as set forth in the most current issue of "Best's Insurance Guide." Licensee shall deliver to Licensor, prior to the Commencement Date, original certificates evidencing the existence and amounts of such insurance. No such policy shall be cancelable or subject to reduction of coverage except after sixty (60) days prior written notice to Licensor. Licensee

shall, within thirty (30) days prior to the expiration, cancellation or reduction of such policies, furnish Licensor with renewals or "binders" thereof. Licensee shall not do or permit to be done anything which shall invalidate the insurance policies required under this Agreement. The limits of such insurance shall not limit Licensee's liability nor relieve Licensee of any obligation hereunder. Licensor shall be named as an additional insured on said policies. The policy shall contain cross-liability endorsements, if applicable. Licensee shall at Licensee's expense, maintain such other liability insurance as Licensee deems necessary to protect Licensee. The certificate shall name [ ]. as additional insured on Licensee's policy.

c) Licensee hereby releases and waives any and all rights of recovery from all Licensor Parties (as defined in Paragraph 9 below) its directors, officers, employees and agents for any loss of damage, including consequential loss or damage, caused by any peril or perils (including negligent acts) that are enumerated in such insurance policies. Such insurance policies shall also contain an express waiver of any and all rights of subrogation thereunder whatsoever against Licensor, its directors, officers, employees and agents.

9. <u>Indemnification</u>. Licensee shall indemnify and hold Licensor, its manager, and their respective corporate affiliates, officers, partners, directors, employees, servants, tenants, contractors, guests, invitees and agents ("Licensor Parties"), and the Property harmless from any and all claims, demands, causes of action, judgments, liabilities, losses, costs, expenses (including attorneys' fees and court costs), liens, charges and encumbrances of any kind whatsoever in connection with, arising out of or by reason of the use of the Property by Licensee, its customers of business invitees;

or in connection with the removal and/or storage of any property on the Property, whether of Licensee or any third party whomsoever, as specified in Section 12, below; or in connection with, arising out of or by reason of any act, omission or negligence of Licensee, its directors, officers, employees, agents, contractors, licensee's, customers or business invitees while in, upon, about or in any way connected with the Property or arising from any accident, injury or damage, howsoever caused, to any person or property whatsoever occurring in, upon, about or in any way connected with the Property. Licensee shall, at its sole cost and expense, obtain the discharge and release of any lien, charge or encumbrance filed of record, within fifteen (15) days after the filing of the same, unless Licensee elects to contest such lien, charge or encumbrance, in which event Licensee shall obtain a release thereof five (5) business days prior to the date such lien would become final. Nothing contained herein shall prevent Licensor, at the cost and for the account of Licensee, from at any time obtaining such discharge and release in the event Licensee shall fail or refuse to do so. Notwithstanding the foregoing, Licensee shall not be required to defend, save harmless or indemnify Licensor from any liability for injury, loss, accident or damage to any person or property resulting from Licensor's gross negligence or willful acts or omissions, or those of Licensor's officers, or employees. Licensee's indemnity is not intended to nor shall it relieve any insurance carrier of its obligations under policies required to be carried by Licensee pursuant to the provisions of this Agreement to the extent that such policies cover the results of grossly negligent acts or omissions of Licensor, its officers, or employees, or the failure of Licensor to perform any of its material obligations under this Agreement Licensee agrees that none of the Licensor Parties shall have any personal liability for any claims by Licensee and Licensee hereby expressly waives and releases such personal liability on behalf of itself and all persons claiming by, through or under Licensee. Licensee agrees that, notwithstanding anything in this Agreement and/or any applicable law to the contrary, the liability of the Licensor Parties, and any recourse by Licensee against the Licensor Parties shall be limited solely and exclusively to Licensee's actual direct damages, but not consequential damages (including but not limited to loss of profits, loss of business opportunity, loss of goodwill or loss of use, in each case however occurring), therefor and shall be recoverable only from the interest of Licensor in the Property.

10. Assignment. Licensee shall not assign or transfer this Agreement or mortgage, pledge, hypothecate or encumber the rights granted herein without the prior written consent of Licensor, nor shall this Agreement inure to the benefit of any trustee in bankruptcy, receiver or other successor of Licensee, whether by operation of law or otherwise, without such consent. Any attempt to assign or transfer this Agreement without such consent shall be null and void and of no force or effect. Licensor shall have the right to assign this Agreement and delegate all or any portion of its duties hereunder to any entity that is the purchaser of all or substantially all the assets of Licensor or to any entity that is the successor to Licensor or merger, consolidation or otherwise, or that is an affiliate of Licensor. This Agreement shall inure to the benefit of and be binding upon the parties hereto and their respective heirs, successors and assignees.

11. Right of Entry. Licensor and its authorized agents and representatives may enter the Property at any time for any purpose. Licensor may place upon the Property signs or plaques giving notice to the effect that the Property is the property of Licensor.

12. Breach; Cancellation. In the event of any breach of any representation contained herein or other default by

Licensee in the performance of any term or condition of this Agreement, in addition to all other rights, remedies, defenses, claims, damages (including, without limitation, punitive and consequential damages), causes of action and equitable relief provided by applicable law, Licensor may forthwith cancel this Agreement, revoke the license granted hereby and re-enter the Property and take possession thereof and remove all persons and property therefrom. Licensee agrees to hold Licensor harmless from any liability whatsoever for the removal and/or storage of any property on the Property, whether of Licensee or any third party whomsoever. This Agreement shall not be construed to limit or waive any of Licensor's rights, remedies claims, defenses, damages (including, without limitation, punitive and consequential damages), causes of action, as permitted by law or equity.

13. <u>Notices</u>.

    a) Any and all notices and demands by or from Licensor to Licensee, or by or from Licensee to Licensor, required or desired to be given hereunder shall be in writing and shall be validly given or made if served either personally or if deposited in the United States mail, certified or registered, postage prepaid, return receipt requested. If such notice or demand be served by registered or certified mail in the manner provided, service shall be conclusively deemed given two (2) days after mailing or upon receipt, whichever is sooner.

    TO Licensor: [NAME]

    TO Licensee: [NAME]

    b) Any party hereto may change its address for the purpose of receiving notices or demands as herein provided by a written notice given in the manner aforesaid to the other party hereto, which notice of change of address shall not become effective, however, until the actual receipt thereof by the other party.

c) All notices hereunder shall be as specific as reasonably necessary to enable the party receiving the same to respond thereto.

14. No Partnership. Nothing contained in this Agreement shall be deemed or construed by the parties hereto or by any third party to create the relationship of principal and agent, master/servant, or of partnership or of joint venture of any association between Licensor and Licensee. No provision of this Agreement, nor any acts of the parties hereto, shall be deemed to create any relationship between Licensor and Licensee other than relationship of licensor and licensee.

15. No Waiver. Licensor's failure to enforce or delay in the enforcement of any provision hereof or any right hereunder shall not be construed as a waiver of such provision or right nor shall it limit or restrain Licensor's exercise thereafter of the same or any other right. This Section 15 may not be waived.

16. Remedies Cumulative. The various rights, options, elections and remedies of Licensor contained in this Agreement shall be cumulative, and no one of them shall be construed as exclusive of any other, or of any right, priority or remedy allowed or provided for by law and not expressly waived in this Agreement.

17. Captions. The captions appearing at the commencement of the sections hereof are descriptive only and for convenience in reference to this Agreement and in no way

whatsoever define, limit or describe the scope or intent of this Agreement, nor in any way effect this Agreement.

18. <u>Governing Law</u>. The laws of the State of [NAME OF STATE shall govern the validity, construction performance and effect of this Agreement.

19. <u>Schedules</u>. Schedules A, B, C, D referred to herein above are acknowledged by Licensee to have been fully and correctly completed and attached hereto prior to the execution of this Agreement, and Licensee agrees that such schedules form a part of this Agreement, and Licensee agrees that such schedules form a part of, and are incorporated in, this Agreement.

20. <u>Security Deposit</u>. On execution of this Agreement, Licensee shall deposit with [NAME OF LOCATION OWNER] $[AMOUNT] as a security deposit for performance by Licensee of the provisions of this Agreement. If Licensee is in default or responsible for any additional fees or costs (including, without limitation, the costs of repairing any damage caused by Licensee or for removing any trash or other materials left by Licensee or clean up costs), Licensor can use the security deposit, or any portion of it, to cure the default or compensate Licensor for any and all damage sustained by Licensor as a result of Licensee's default. Licensee shall immediately upon demand pay to The Hollywood Location Company, Agent for Licensor, a sum equal to the portion of the security deposit expended or applied by Licensor as provided herein so as to maintain the security deposit in the sum initially deposited with The Hollywood Location Company. If Licensee is not in default at the expiration or the termination of this Agreement, The Hollywood Location Company shall return the security deposit to Licensee. The Hollywood Location Company' obligations with respect to the security deposit are those

of a debtor and not a trustee. The Hollywood Location Company can maintain the security deposit separate and apart from Licensor's general funds or can commingle the security deposit with The Hollywood Location Company' general and other funds. The Hollywood Location Company shall not be required to pay Licensee interest on the security deposit. Licensee waives any claims against Licensor for any use of the Security Deposit by The Hollywood Location Company.

21. <u>Personnel</u>. In the event that Licensor, in its sole discretion and benefit, determines that security personnel or engineers or other contractors will be required with respect to the use of the Property by Licensee, Licensee shall immediately pay to [NAME OF LOCATION OWNER] for the services of these individuals, the following:

(a) Security Personnel: $[per hour]

(b) OTHER PERSONNEL: $[AMOUNT]

22. <u>Location Representative</u>. Licensor may require that its Location Representative be present on all prep/film/strike days at the following rates:

$[ ] per hour - first Eight (8) hours on weekdays
$[ ] per hour - after Eight (8) hours on weekdays or first Eight (8) hours on weekends or holidays
$[ ] per hour - after Twelve (12) hours on weekdays or after Eight (8) hours on weekends or holidays

23. <u>Special Effects</u>. Licensee may not use any special effects, pyrotechnics, or smoke effects without the prior written consent of the Licensor in advance of such use.

24. Duration.

(a) A "preparation day" and "strike day" are any day other than a "filming day" or "holding day," as defined below, upon which Licensee conducts construction, installation, dismantling, restoration or removal operations in the License Area.

(b) A "filming day" is any day upon which Licensee conducts video or film photography or recording, or both, in the License Area. Any day designated a "filming day" shall be considered such by the parties whether the camera rolls or not.

(c) A "holding day" is any day other than a "preparation day," "strike day" or "filming day," on which the License Area is occupied by Licensee's personnel, equipment or both.

A preparation day and strike day shall be considered Twelve (12) hours and filming day shall be considered Three (3) hours. Licensee's use of the License Area for longer than Twelve (12) on Prep and Strike days and longer than Three (3) hours Shoot days will be considered overtime and will entail an increase in the License Fee. This amount is $[ ] per hour on Prep and Strike days and $[ ] per hour on Shoot days.

25. Rights to Project and Film. Subject to any existing right, title and interest of any third parties from which no enforceable releases are obtained, neither Licensor nor anyone claiming through Licensor shall have any right, title or interest in or to Licensee's photography and recordings made on the Property, nor shall there be any restriction or limitation on Licensee's right to use such photography and recordings, in the Property or any exploitation, exhibition or

advertising thereof, or any other of Licensee's productions; in any and all media, whether now known or hereafter devised, throughout the universe, in perpetuity. .

26. Entire Agreement. This Agreement sets forth the entire understanding and agreement between the parties hereto and supersedes all previous communications, negotiations and agreements, whether oral or written, with respect to the subject matter hereof. No addition to or modification of this Agreement shall be binding on either party unless reduced to writing. No representation or statement not expressly contained in this Agreement or in any written, properly executed amendment to this Agreement shall be binding upon Licensor or Licensee as a warranty or otherwise.

IN WITNESS WHEREOF, the parties hereto have caused this Agreement to be executed the day of , 20_.

Licensor: **Licensee:**

By: By: ___

Its: Its: ___

Schedule A

The area(s) being utilized for the filming/video shall be as follows-[DESCRIPTION]

Schedule B

As consideration for Licensee's use of the Property during the Term, Licensee shall pay to Licensor the following:

	# of Days	Daily Rate	Total
Prep Day(s)	0	$	$
Shoot Day(s)	1	$	$
Strike Day(s)	0	$	$
Hold Day(s)	0	$	$
Total Days:	1	Total License Fee:	$

*The Total License Fee shall be paid by [TIME - AM/PM on DATE]. Payment shall be in the form of a company check or cashier's check payable to [ ].

Schedule C

The purpose of this license is for [NAME OF PRODUCTION COMPANY] to engage in production of a [DESCRIPTION OF SHOOT entitled "[NAME OF PRODUCTION]".

Schedule D

Prep Dates and Times:

Shoot Dates and Times:

Strike Dates and Times:

Hold Dates and Times:

* Specific times of use to be determined.

CHAPTER 8

ARTWORK RELEASE FORM

Artwork Release Form Chapter Notes

If you are creating a video and you decide to show any artwork such as a painting, poster, sculpture, drawing, etc. where the copyright is not owned by you then you will need to sign a release. It is always best to avoid using any material protected by copyright.

The copyright owner of the artwork must sign a release form giving you the permission to include their work in a video.

Artwork Release Form

From: -[NAME AND ADDRESS OF PRODUCTION COMPANY]

[NAME OF VIDEO PROJECT]

[DATE]

Dear_____,For good and valuable consideration the receipt of which is hereby acknowledged, I, the Artist (defined below), do hereby irrevocably grant the right and license to the unlimited use of my Artwork (defined below) by Producer (defined below) and their affiliated companies, successors, assigns and licensees for use and display in the Video (defined below), which Video may be displayed and/or broadcast for any purpose in any and all media now known or hereafter developed throughout the world, without limitation as to duration or frequency of use. I represent that I am the author of and owner of all rights in and to the Artwork and that I have the sole and exclusive right to make the within grant of rights, including but not limited to moral rights, that neither I nor anyone else has any contractual or other arrangements which will interfere with rights herein granted and warrant that the rights herein granted will not infringe on the rights of any third party and that the consent or permission of no other party is required by Producer, its successors, assigns or licensees in connection with the use of the Artwork. I agree to indemnify and hold Producer and its divisions, subsidiaries, affiliates, officers, directors, agents, employees, successors, assigns and licensees harmless from and against any and all liabilities, damages, suits and expenses (including reasonable attorney's fees and disbursements) arising out of or in connection with the breach or alleged breach of any representation and/or warranty made hereunder. The Producer, its successors, assigns and licensees shall have the right to alter, edit, modify, adapt, reproduce and illustrate (as appropriate) the Artwork for any use. All right, title and interest in and to the Video incorporating the Artwork shall be vested in Producer and any of its subsidiary and affiliated companies, successors, assigns and licensees. I waive any inspection or approval of the finished material and I release Producer and any of its subsidiary and affiliated companies, successors, assigns and licensees from any liability for any claim of alteration, optical illusion or faulty mechanical reproduction. This agreement constitutes the entire understanding between the undersigned and Producer with respect to the subject matter herein. Any waiver, modification or addition to this agreement shall not be valid unless in writing and signed by both parties.

Agreed and Accepted:
Signature of Artist _____
Print Name of Artist _____
Artist's Email & Physical Address _____
Title of Artwork _____

Signature of Producer _____

CHAPTER 9

COMPOSER AGREEMENT

Composer Agreement Chapter Notes

A key element of any composer agreement is whether the composer will be responsible for recording the music as well as writing the music and who owns the rights. The composer agreement in this chapter is considered a "work for hire" document whereby the content producer or production company owns all rights including both the underlying music and the recording of that music.

This form of agreement gives the content producer or production company full control of the music and enables them to use it where and how they choose. It sets out the basic relationship, payment terms, duties and obligations between the content producer and the composer.

COMPOSER AGREEMENT

This Agreement is made and effective as of [DATE], (the "Effective Date") between [NAME OF PRODUCER/ PRODUCTION COMPANY], ("Producer") and [NAME OF COMPOSER] (the "Composer") in connection with the original musical score for [NAME OF PROJECT/ VIDEO]. ("Video").

1. SERVICES. Producer hereby engages Composer to compose, arrange, orchestrate, conduct, produce, prepare, package, record, perform, and deliver an original musical score (the "Score") for the Video. The Score shall include the underlying musical compositions for each underscore cue (collectively the "Compositions") and all master recordings of the Compositions (collectively the "Masters"). Composer shall render to Producer in connection with the Video and in accordance with Producer's instructions and requests all services customarily rendered by Composer in connection with composing, arranging, orchestrating. conducting, recording, and producing original musical scores for the Video. Composer's services shall be on an exclusive basis through delivery and acceptance of the Masters of the Score.

2. SCHEDULE. Composer's services should commence upon full execution of this Agreement or on such date as Producer designates, which shall continue until completion of all services required by Producer hereunder. Composer shall deliver the Masters to Producer in such form(s) as Producer shall require, on such date(s) as Producer shall designate. Time of delivery is of the essence to this Agreement.

3. COMPENSATION. Provided that Composer fully and satisfactorily performs all obligations, and is not in breach of any duties, obligations, representations, or warranties set forth herein, then Composer shall be entitled to receive [$ AMOUNT] ("Composer Fee"), out of which Composer shall be solely responsible to pay Composer's own personal costs incurred in composing and performing the Score and producing, recording, and delivering the Masters, including all costs associated with the hiring and employment of Composer's assistant (if any), and all equipment and rental costs, and further including all fees and costs of any and all contributors to the Score, including any and all artists, musicians, technicians, studio costs, and recording producers as will be required for recording the Score

Composer Fee is payable as follows:

    3.1 [$ AMOUNT] upon signature of this agreement;

    3.2 [AMOUNT] upon Composer's completion and satisfactory delivery of the Score and Producer's acceptance of all services and work product hereunder.

4. CREDIT. If Composer fully performs all of Composer's services hereunder, and is not in breach or default hereunder, Producer shall accord Composer credit in substantially as follows:

"Music by [NAME OF COMPOSER] " or "Composed by [NAME OF COMPOSER]"

5. MASTER RIGHTS.

> 5.1 Producer is and shall be the sole and exclusive copyright owner (including without limitation, all renewals and extensions of copyrights) and owner of all rights of every kind and nature whatsoever in and to the Masters and shall be considered a full buyout of all such rights.

6. COMPOSITION RIGHTS.

> a. Subject to the provisions hereunder, Composer and Producer agree that the Producer shall exclusively own and control all copyrights and music publishing rights in and to the Compositions, which collectively comprise the Score. Notwithstanding the foregoing, Composer shall grant the Producer (its successors, licensees, and assigns) an irrevocable, royalty-free synchronization, performance, and mechanical license with respect to each Composition in connection with the Video and the promotion thereof, and any subsequent or ancillary works based in whole or in part on the Video , in perpetuity throughout the universe in all online digital media including Producer's client's website or affiliated sites or any other online media or internet environments. Since this agreement sets out a full buyout of all rights the Producer is also not responsible for any public performance rights including but not limited to ASCAP, BMI and/or SESAC.

7. ASSIGNMENT. Producer shall have the right to assign this Agreement and all or any part of Producer's rights hereunder in whole or in part to any person or entity.

8. REMEDIES. No breach by Producer of any provision hereof shall give Composer the right to injunctive or other equitable relief with respect to, or otherwise to interfere in any way with the production, promotion, advertisement, distribution, sale, lease, license or other exploitation of the Score, the Video, or any other materials contemplated hereunder. Composer's sole remedy for any such breach shall be limited to an action at law to seek money damages, if any.

9. MISCELLANEOUS. This Agreement constitutes the entire agreement of the parties hereto with respect to the subject matter hereof and shall not be modified except by written document executed by Composer and Producer. Section headings in this Agreement are for convenience only and shall not be used in the interpretation or construction of this Agreement The validity, construction, interpretation, and legal effect of this Agreement shall be governed by the laws of the state of [NAME OF STATE]. This Agreement shall be binding upon and shall inure to the benefit of the parties hereto and their respective heirs, successors, and permissible assigns. This Agreement contains the full understanding of the parties and supersedes all prior agreements and understandings, whether written or oral, pertaining thereto.

Agreed and Accepted
The parties have executed this agreement.

For and On Behalf of [NAME OF PRODUCER/ PRODUCTION COMPANY]

_____

For and on behalf of the Composer

_____

CHAPTER 10

MUSIC LICENSE

Music License Agreement Chapter Notes

Music is one of the most essential elements in the creation of content. It can also be a very complex and specialized task to clear certain types of music for inclusion in your work. Content creators should understand that when using music there are two rights to every song.
1. The person who wrote the song may hold the "publisher rights" also known as the "sync rights".
2. The person who recorded the song will hold the "master rights"

To use a song, you will need permission from both entities. Once you determine who owns the publishing and master rights you will need to contact them separately and ask for permission to use the song.

Once you have figured this out, you will now have to decide what sort of usage you will need for the music in your work. This is often refereed to as the "scope of rights". Is it for a film, television show, tv commercial, internet only ad? How long do you need the music for? Do you want to have an exclusive right to use it for a period of time and for a certain category of products? These are all questions that will come up when considering licensing music for your production.

To make things more difficult, if the music you wish to use is well known and popular it may be expensive to use and the owners may not give you the right to use it in your content.

For content makers, it is always easier to find music that you can license once and use the music as long as you want.

There are many companies that offer low cost music or royalty free music that you can pay a one-time fee and use the music however you want in as many projects as you like without the need to purchase additional licenses. The use of the music will depend on the actual license terms that the supplier negotiates with the content producer.

MUSIC LICENSE AGREEMENT

Dated as of: _____

Producer/Production Company

Client: - [NAME OF CLIENT] (hereafter "Licensee")

Supplier/Composer- [NAME OF COMPOSER/SUPPLIER OF MUSIC ("hereafter "Supplier")

Composition(s)/Sound Recording(s)

Supplier provided: -[NAME OF TRACK/SONG]

Production(s)

License Fee: [AMOUNT OF LICENSE FEE]

License Commencement Date: [DATE]

In consideration of the License Fee set forth above to be paid upon presentation of invoice by Supplier to Producer, as agent to Client, Supplier hereby agrees to grant Licensee the rights to the Composition(s)/Sound Recording(s) as set forth in this Agreement on the following terms of conditions:

1. GRANT OF RIGHTS

The Licensee is entitled to the exclusive use of the Composition(s)/Sound Recording(s) for the purpose of advertising Client's products and/or services for all uses and on broadcast of all platforms for distribution now known or hereafter invented within the following geographic territory,(Worldwide) (hereafter the "Licensed Territory") for a period of [twelve (12) months]. (hereafter the "Initial Term"). The Supplier acknowledges that the Licensee shall have the exclusive right in the [NAME OF CATEGORY IF APPLICABLE] category during the Initial Term.

At the expiry of the initial term the Client will have the non-exclusive right in perpetuity for the purposes of advertising and promoting the client's products and services. The Supplier acknowledges that no further payments other than those set out in this agreement shall be paid for the use of the Compositions/Sound Recordings

> Supplier shall remain the sole owner of the Composition(s)/Sound Recording(s) as well as all publishing rights pertaining to the Composition. Licensee understands and agrees that Supplier has retained all public performance rights (SESAC) in the musical recording and arrangements thereof, that this agreement does not transfer any public performance rights in the musical recording, and that any performance of this music will be licensed in accordance with the rules and regulations of the applicable public performance organization.

> Except for those rights granted above the Licensee acknowledges and agrees that Supplier is the sole and exclusive owner of all rights, including copyright, in and to the Composition(s)/Sound Recording(s) described

above. Furthermore, Licensee hereby irrevocably transfers, on behalf of itself, its employees and agents, to Supplier, any and all rights that it, its employees or agents, may have in the Composition(s)/Sound Recording(s) described above as a result of any contribution they may have made to such Composition(s)/Sound Recording(s). Licensee shall not claim, use or dispose of any rights in the music or lyrics or any portion thereof, and Licensee shall receive no rights in such music or lyrics, other than those granted specifically in this Agreement.

Licensee shall not reproduce the Composition(s)/Sound Recording(s) in any format for direct sale or license to third parties such as compact discs, digital downloads, or digital streams.

2. **WARRANTIES AND REPRESENTATION**
   Supplier warrants and represents that:

   a. it is the sole author of the Composition(s)/Sound Recordings or has otherwise acquired all ownership rights in the Composition(s)/Sound Recording(s); ;

   b. it has no knowledge of any infringement or violation of copyrights or any other rights of any person or entity imposed by the Composition(s)/Sound Recording(s).

   c. no adverse claim exists with respect to the Composition(s)/Sound Recording(s);;

   d. no assignment or pledge have been made of any rights in the Composition(s)/Sound Recording(s); ;

   e. Supplier has the full right, power, and authority to make and enter into this Agreement, and the rights granted to Licensee hereunder will not violate the legal or equitable rights of any third party.

Notwithstanding the foregoing, Licensee understands and agrees that Supplier has made no independent investigation as to whether or not any person, persons or company in the Licensed Territory is currently using, or has used, to identify their products or services, a lyric, slogan, or theme similar to the one performed for Licensee on the Composition(s)/Sound Recording(s). It is specifically understood that Licensee shall not use any lyric, slogan or theme in the licensed territory if such use would violate the trademark or rights of any other person, persons or company.

3. **INDEMNITY**

    Each party hereby agrees to and do hereby indemnify, save and hold the other party and their affiliates and licensees harmless from any and all claims, losses, and damages (including court costs and reasonable attorney's fees) arising out of, connected with or as a result of any inconsistency with, failure of, or breach by it of any warranty, representation, agreement, undertaking, or covenant contained in this agreement including, without limitation, any claim by any third party in connection with the foregoing. In addition to any other rights or remedies the non-breaching parties may have by reason of such inconsistency, failure, breach, threatened breach or claim, the breaching party shall promptly reimburse the non-breaching party, on demand, for any payment made by the non-breaching party after the date hereof with respect to any loss, damage, or liability resulting directly therefrom. Each party shall give the other notice of any third-party claim to which the foregoing indemnity applies and the non-breaching party shall have the right to participate in the defence of any such claim. This paragraph 3 shall also apply to the warranties and representations made by Producer to Supplier in paragraph 2 of this agreement.

4. NO WAIVER

The failure of either party to exercise rights granted upon the occurrence of any of the contingencies set forth in this Agreement shall not in any event constitute a waiver of such rights upon the recurrence of any such contingencies.

5. NOTICES

Any notices given with respect to this Agreement will be in writing and delivered by certified or registered mail, postage pre-paid, to Licensee or Supplier, as the case may be. Said notice will be deemed to have been given two (2) days after deposit.

6. APPLICABLE LAW

This agreement and all matters or issues collateral thereto shall be governed by the laws of the State of [NAME OF STATE] applicable to contracts made and to be performed entirely therein.

7. COMPLETE AGREEMENT

This document constitutes the entire understanding between the parties with respect to the subject matter hereof and supersedes all prior agreements. No waiver, modification or addition to this Agreement shall be valid unless in writing and signed by the parties hereto.

8. **ATTORNEY FEES AND COSTS:**
   Should any action be brought for damages or to enforce or interpret this Agreement, the prevailing party shall be entitled to reasonable attorney's fees and costs.

NAME OF COMPOSER/ SUPPLIER	Licensee: **NAME OF PRODUCER** (Producer on behalf of Client)
By: _____ Signature:_____	Name: Title

CHAPTER 11

SAMPLE CALL SHEET

Call Sheet

DATE		LOCATION		WEATHER
Production Office				

PRODUCTION CELLS			CREW PARKING		NEAREST HOSPITAL

NOTES

GENERAL CREW CALL:	
BREAKFAST:	
LUNCH:	

PRODUCTION SUMMARY	
PRODUCTION CALL	
GENERAL CREW CALL	
1st Shot	
LUNCH	
CAM. WRAP.	
CREW WRAP	

CREW

DESCRIPTION	NAME	PHONE	EMAIL	CALL	WRAP

CLIENT

NAME	PHONE	E-MAIL	CALL

TALENT

CAMERA

MAKEUP/COSTUME

SET DESIGN

LOCATION AND CATERING

www.ingramcontent.com/pod-product-compliance
Lightning Source LLC
Chambersburg PA
CBHW031433210526
45464CB00005B/2178